All about Elcom

All about Elcombe

The intimate history of a Cotswold hamlet

ROBIN SHARP

WYGESTY PUBLISHING

First published in 2003
by Wygesty Publishing

Copyright © 2003 by Robin Sharp
All rights reserved.

British Library Cataloguing-in-Publication Data:
A catalogue record for this book is available from the British Library

ISBN 0-9544317-0-7

Wygesty Publishing
5 Harrowby Court
Harrowby Street
London W1H 5FA

Designed by Lee Young.
Origination and typesetting
in Perpetua by Slad Valley Press.

Printed on Munken Print Extra 115gsm a chlorine-free Swedish
paper which fulfils the requirements of the Nordic Eco-label.
The cover paper is *Bier-Ale,* made from hops, malt and recycled beer labels.

Cover illustration: Clifford Harper
Photographs on pp. 3, 33, 34, 40, 43, 48, 69, 72, 96(b), 98,
99, 107, 108, 119(b), 127, 133 by the author

Printed in Great Britain

For Leonora and Fabian

Acknowledgments

All the people the author could find with knowledge or memories of Elcombe have contributed to this book. In a real sense, therefore, it is theirs as much as his. The only regret will be if others have been missed who could have added more.

Invaluable help has come from many past and present residents of the hamlet, especially in commenting on the first draft and correcting a number of mistakes it contained. For this, special thanks are due to Janet Bartlett, whose diligence in checking many facts has been greatly appreciated, and to all those (some no longer with us) who gave their time unstintingly for interviews. In particular, John Myles, John Papworth, Peter and Joan Shillito and Richard Morris have provided significant contributions and welcome encouragement in the task of compiling this tiny fragment of England's social history.

For the book as a thing in itself, which aspires to be as pleasing to the senses as the place it represents, warm thanks are due to Lee Young, who designed it, and to Jim Clarke of Slad Valley Press. And lastly but not leastly, a hug and a kiss for Cicci, who, apart from her perceptive critique of the text, has allowed the research and writing to take up more time than some might have considered reasonable.

Contents

Preface		ix
1	Origins – *From earliest times to 1200 AD*	1
2	The first 700 years – *1200-1900 AD*	11
3	Dramatic transformations – *The 20th Century*	23
4	The lie of the land – *A walking tour*	35
5	Five generations, 25 children – *The Bartlett Family*	45
6	The last of the old-timers – *Bill Tuck*	49
7	'The greatest man in England' – *R H Tawney*	55
8	When Harry met Tutu – *Jeanette Tawney*	61
9	'A funny old cocker' – *John Papworth*	73
10	Around the houses – *The cottages and the people*	81
11	Property at issue – *Not in my back yard!*	125
12	The Future – *A little fantasy*	133
Sources and further reading		137
Index		138

Vignettes

The emperor's hors d'oeuvre	7
Riches of history on our doorstep	15
Crime and violence	21
Flora and fauna	29
Buried treasure	41
A very special goat – and other pets	48
On Shanks's pony	70
Sneeze up a tree	85
The gypsy caravan	90
'An unlabelled can of beans'	98
That sinking feeling - nearly	103
A new lake for Caragh	106
wwwelcome to elcombe	129
The sound of silence	131

Preface

This little book is the fruit of intermittent efforts over nearly 20 years to piece together something of the history of Elcombe. Being such a tiny community, with scarce a dozen houses, and having been peopled for its first five centuries by unlettered farm labourers who left little record of their lives, one might think this should have been a task of months, not years. But the story of Elcombe reaches out in many directions, and endeavouring to sort out the multifarious strands has sometimes been a bit like trying to eat spaghetti with boxing gloves.

The result is an assemblage of facts, impressions, opinions, hearsay, sentiments and memories – many of them uncheckable, most of them quite subjective, but which together may give a truer image of this special place than would be possible in a work of more rigorous scholarship. That, at any rate, is the hope. The more particular aims have been, first, to bring together in one place much scattered knowledge and information about Elcombe's past, and secondly, to preserve some of the more recent, undocumented and human-scale reality of people's lives, which would otherwise soon be forgotten and lost.

Other settlements may have taken the name Elcombe, but this one, high on the eastern slopes of the beautiful Slad Valley, has had the name for some 700 years. In all that time, its most radical transformation has occurred in the past half-century – a microcosm of what has happened to so many villages throughout the Cotswolds.

This is an 'intimate history' in the sense of seeking to convey something of the context of people's individual lives. Going back only a generation or two into a world of poverty and the pains of untreated ill-health, one would be tempted to say that suicide in Elcombe was part of the way of life. But here we are concerned with the human stories, not statistics. And there are other kinds of intimacy: the childless architect writing stories for his neighbours' children; the genteel but spendthrift professor's wife constantly seeking financial help from her rich brother. The story of Elcombe upto AD 2000 has been a modest but colourful pageant.

R.S.
Whiteway, October 2002

I ORIGINS
From earliest times to 1200 AD

It's a summer evening around 1918 and a young girl is coming home from playing in the fields, the brim of her straw hat encircled with a ribbon of lights. One can imagine her friends laughing at this ring of luminous green around her head, which pulsates in the twilight – for it is a ribbon of glowworms. It is also one of the memorable moments of an Elcombe childhood. The girl still remembered it more than 60 years later. "There were swarms of glowworms in the hedgerows then" – and she had quickly collected enough to garland her hat. Nowadays, she knew, it was hard to find more than one or two glowworms blinking their messages through the dusk, but then there were so many.

A sadder memory of those years for Gwen Fern, living with her mother and younger brother at Yew Tree Cottage, was that her father had been killed in the trenches of World War I. He was serving as a private in the Somerset Light Infantry and his name is preserved on the Slad War Memorial.

Coming back from the fields, that day or another, Gwen Fern would have passed the top of King Charles' Lane, now hardly more than a muddy track through the woods but once a main thoroughfare. And there she would have been connected, even if unwittingly, with three moments of Elcombe's history spanning 130,000 millennia. Like children before and since, she will have bent to pick up a curiously shaped piece of stone and found that it contained small marine fossils: the remains of life from 130 million years ago, when Elcombe and the Cotswold escarpment in which it nestles were all under the sea. At the top of the lane, where it joins the since tarmacked road to Bisley at a steep hairpin bend, unknown to Gwen she was passing within a few feet of the grave of the earliest human we now know to have ended his days in Elcombe. The bones of a late Neolithic man, buried with his

[1]

dog about 4,000 years ago, were only discovered some years later. The third moment of history that her walk retraced was one that everyone at Elcombe knows – that August day in 1643 when, in the midst of England's civil war, King Charles I brought his army this way through the woods on his way to try to finish the siege of Gloucester. Maybe she imagined she could hear the clatter of horses' hooves echoing from the past as she clambered up the stony track.

Three moments in the story of this little place, with the image of Gwen Fern, skipping through the fields with her luminous ribbon of glowworms, perhaps making a fitting fourth to bring us closer to the present day.

The oolitic limestone which has been the traditional building material for houses in Elcombe, as throughout the Cotswolds, provides a starting-point for the natural history of this place. Oolite is a sedimentary rock (the word means 'egg stone' because its structure is like fish roe) and it was formed about 150 million years ago, when the whole escarpment was under the sea, with layers of fossil-bearing ragstone laid on top of it some 10-15 million years later. Today there are disused quarries at both ends of the hamlet – a large one cut out of Swifts Hill and a smaller one, now hardly visible, at the top of King Charles' Lane – which for centuries must have been the principal resource for house construction.

Over millions of years the seascape became a landscape and eventually early Man made his appearance in what we now call northern Europe, when Elcombe and the rest of Britain were part of the continental landmass. That was perhaps 400,000 years ago, but recurrent ice ages, which pushed them back to the south, meant there could be no permanent settlement. During the cold periods, the inhabitants of this region were mammoth, woolly rhinoceros, bison, wild horse and reindeer. When it was warmer there were elephant, bear, lion, jaguar, sabre-toothed tiger and fallow deer. Homo sapiens arrived in northern Europe about 40,000 years ago. Tools and weapons of that age have been found in Gloucester and on the edge of the escarpment only a few miles from Elcombe. But they were also forced out by the last ice age, which receded only 12,000 years ago.

It is not easy to comprehend the timescale of history from the

Life as it was: marine fossils, 130 million years old, are found in the ragstone all around Elcombe

earliest rock formation to the present. But if one considers that whole span, from then till now, as being one year — and that we are now at midnight on December 31st — then homo sapiens arrived in these parts just three hours ago.

Bands of hunter-gatherers

Until 4000-5000 BC, these first residents were cave-dwelling hunter-gatherers, and the evidence suggests they lived in small bands. They made numerous settlements in the high Cotswolds, and notably in the area between Bisley and Painswick, between 6500 and 3500 BC. Over 40 sites in Gloucestershire have yielded Later Mesolithic flint tools — and since flint was not found locally it seems they must have been trading with other groups as far away as Cornwall or the north of England.

Farming began about 5,500 years ago at the start of the Neolithic period, and within the next millennium there is evidence of a cluster of settlements and related burial monuments, including long barrows, in the Bisley area. On the escarpment a few miles from Elcombe, near present-day Birdlip, there seem to have been two fortified villages at this time. The people were farmers, who prospered and left their mark on the area in the form of forest clearances, causewayed camps and long barrows. The 'Jurassic Way', following the higher ground of the Cotswolds, is known to be an ancient track and may even have been in use at this time.

Hierarchies develop

Then, around 2000 BC the native population – still mostly wandering hunters, pig-keepers and shepherds – began to be overtaken by immigrants of Mediterranean stock. After 2,500 BC hierarchies and disparities of wealth began to develop, leading to conflicts which may also have been due to competition for land or food shortages. One way or another, the Cotswold uplands appear to have been abandoned for 1,000 years, with no evidence of new settlements in the Bisley area until a climatic improvement brought warmer, drier conditions in the early Bronze Age (after 1600 BC). But a few hundred years later the climate changed again (colder, wetter) and people again retreated to the

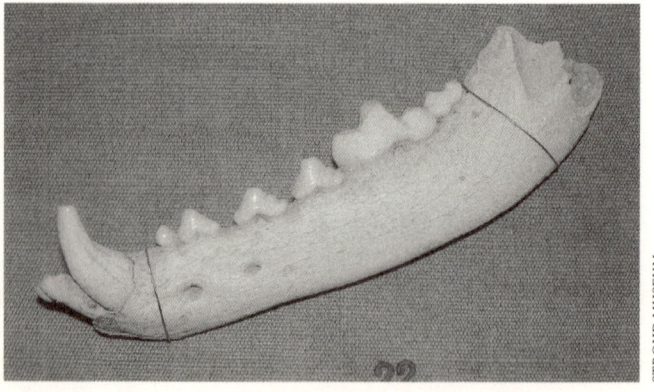

This dog's jawbone of the Late Neolithic period was discovered in a shallow pit along with numerous human bones - the earliest evidence of a human presence at Elcombe

valleys. There were no new settlements around Bisley from 700 to 300 BC, after which – with the arrival of the Iron Age Celts – a number of hillforts were built in the region (300-100BC), including the substantial Kimbury Fort at Painswick Beacon. Pollen analysis shows that by now there were fewer trees and more grassland, suggesting a predominance of sheep in some areas.

The Celts were fairer-skinned and taller than the people they superseded; they had many gods and an organised priesthood, and one of their tribes, the Dobunni, made its capital a few miles away near Cirencester.

At the time of the Roman conquest, the people of the Cotswolds were mostly farmers, though there were probably some full-time craftsmen as well as privileged classes of leaders and priests. Unable to match the fighting strength of the Roman legionaries, the dissident Celts were forced to retreat westward into Wales or Cornwall. The Romans stationed a cavalry unit at Cirencester (Corinium) and another army unit near Gloucester (Glevum) to protect their frontier against the Welsh – roughly along the line of the later Fosse Way. When they pulled back from these bases only 50 years later (100AD), they left behind much-enlarged civilian settlements, their occupation having improved the standard of living for many local people.

The landscape

After the upheavals earlier in our historic "year", the topography of the Slad Valley and the Cotswolds in general has altered little in the last 45 minutes – that is, the last 10,000 years. On the other hand, there have been dramatic changes in the soil and vegetation. Soon after the end of the last ice age, which left our land an offshore island of Europe for the first time, all of southern Britain was covered with woodland. This resulted in thick, humus-rich soils providing browsing for many animals and in due course good ground for crops.

Major woodland clearances appear to have started around 1750BC, which is also the date of the first cereal pollens found. By 400BC large areas of land had been cleared, creating the basis of the man-made 'countryside' that we like to think of as being natural. In those times the early farmers relied on a mix of livestock and crops: cattle, pigs, sheep, wheat and barley, supplemented by hunting and fishing and wild fruits and nuts. Unfortunately, over the next 2000 years the woodland clearances and the agriculture that followed led to drastic erosion of the soil, so that by the time William Cobbett made his 'Rural Rides' around England in the early 1800s, he found the land of Gloucestershire to offer only a poor stone-brash.

A human presence

For Elcombe, pre-history lasted until some 4000 years ago, when we have the first sure evidence of a human presence in this part of the Slad

Valley. In 1936, Jeanette Tawney, who was then living at Rose Cottage, encountered one day a Council workman who had unearthed some bones in a quarry near her home: to be precise, where King Charles' Lane meets the hairpin bend. He was going to throw them away, but Mrs Tawney persuaded him to let her take them to Stroud Museum for analysis. They turned out to be the bones of a man (or perhaps two men) and a dog, apparently buried together. On 10th September she wrote to her brother: "The Curator of the Stroud Museum sent them to the British Museum, who sent them to the College of Surgeons, who have pronounced them to be Neolithic Late – i.e. 4,000 years ago." One of the numerous bones found is now on display at Stroud's new Museum in the Park, but the rest appear to have been lost in the old museum's disorganised stores.

After Mrs Tawney's discovery, a museum official visited the quarry and reported afterwards that "many bones were obtained, but no skull". His account in the Proceedings of the Cotteswold Naturalists' Field Club for 1936 says the bones were mostly found adjacent to the quarry in an excavated hollow, three feet six inches deep, resting on a bed of small stones on the floor of the hollow. He says the Royal College of Surgeons concluded that "there are two individuals represented", but he does not make clear whether the dog counted as an individual.

Under the Romans
From that time until the Roman occupation, doubtless the ancient Britons and/or the Celts came through this valley and camped where they could be seen by anyone taking shelter in this high combe. But the next hard evidence of a human presence on these upper slopes of the valley is the two Roman votive tablets found at the Custom Scrubs, a remote, wooded area of the valley two miles from Elcombe. One of the tablets, 19 inches high, depicts Romulus, founder of Rome, and it's believed this was the site of a Roman villa, even though nothing else of it remains. Given the importance of their garrisons at Cirencester only 12 miles to the southeast and at Gloucester on the other side, it is not surprising that some senior Roman officials should have settled this strategic hinterland. Cirencester was the second largest town in Roman Britain and there are the remains of several of their villas within a radius of a few miles.

The emperor's hors d'oeuvre

A delightful series of hand-made booklets for Elcombe's children was produced from the late 1970s by Graham Wenman (Linden & Habricia Cottages). Based on contemporary or historical events in the hamlet, Graham's little stories – which he illustrated with drawings or linocuts – were a charming mixture of fact and fantasy. This one was called "The Emperor's hors d'oeuvre":

LINOCUT, GRAHAM WENMAN

Consul Flavius Vespasian was tired and hungry. He and his officers had led the 2nd Augusta Legion many miles up the Fosse Way from Sarum to Birdlip Hill above Gloucester, but clearly they would not reach their legionary fortress by nightfall. A born soldier, Vespasian insisted upon marching in front of the Standards at the head of his troops. We are told by the historian Tacitus that he dressed like his men and ate the same food.

Unfortunately, he was somewhat mean and tended to 'travel light', preferring to 'live off the land'. He gave orders to make camp for the night, and true to their long-established practice the tough legionnaires 'formed square' and dug a defence ditch for the night. The local 'Dobunii' tribesmen might sound like tame rabbits but they did not always behave so peaceably!

The Consul, later to become one of the most successful Emperors of Imperial Rome, had his mess table set up and was joined by his six Tribunes for dinner.

The quartermaster was apologetic. "I'm sorry gentlemen," he said, "we have only local chicken for the main course and some snails which we confiscated on our way through France for hors d'oeuvre, and red wine."

"Excellent," said the Consul, "we shall eat royally at Glevum tomorrow and save money in the meantime."

Actually, they only had about six snails apiece as, when the cooks opened the crate in the bullock-cart, several young boy and girl snails escaped and hid behind the rocks at the roadside.

And that, I am told, is how the large grey snails, still to be seen in large numbers in the gardens and stone walls of Elcombe, came into existence. The heavy rain and lush local vegetation doubtless increased their size over the past 1500 years.

(This story could be said to be true — at least it is based on a strong local legend, which is that the large grey snails which abound in the Stroud district were actually imported by the Romans. I leave Leonora and Fabian to decide.*)

* *Leonora and Fabian Sharp of Yew Tree Cottage were at the time living in Rome.*

After the Roman withdrawal, the British repulsed waves of Anglo-Saxon attacks upto the year 500AD, but in the 6th century the new invaders pushed progressively westward and after Ceawlin, King of Wessex, won a major battle at Dyrham, near Bath, in 576, Cirencester and Gloucester (and presumably the land in between including Elcombe) came under English rule for the first time. At the end of Ceawlin's reign, the Kingdom of Wessex comprised the modern counties of Berkshire, Hampshire, Wiltshire and a large part of Gloucestershire. By the mid-7th century, most of the Cotswolds were united as the small Kingdom of the Hwicce, forming part of Mercia. And with the Hwicce, Christianity — which previously had only a small number of converts — became established.

The church prospered, to the extent that by the end of the 8th century it is estimated to have owned about one-quarter of all Gloucestershire land. With an educated priesthood, this may be one reason why Anglo-Saxon words have survived in our language much better than British or Norman ones.

Agriculture was by now well diversified, with crops including barley, oats, wheat, rye, hemp, flax, woad, beans and vines. On the livestock side, apart from cows, oxen, pigs and poultry, sheep-farming became an important agro-industry in the Saxon period, laying the foundation for a thousand years of Cotswolds' prosperity. Most houses would have had a loom, and women spent a lot of their time spinning and weaving to make clothes for their families.

According to one source, the population of all Gloucestershire was about 50,000 at this time. However, the much later Domesday Book counted 8,239 adult males, which would suggest a significantly lower total. Whatever the numbers, the overwhelming majority were farm labourers and it is reckoned that as many as 25 per cent were effectively slaves.

Vikings and Normans
The people on the Cotswolds had barely 300 years to get used to their new language and masters, and then in the 9th century came the Vikings. After landing in East Anglia in 865 they conquered Mercia, which included Gloucester, but they failed more than once to defeat King Alfred in Wessex and after regrouping in Gloucester they retreated eventually to settle in East Anglia. By that time Anglo-Saxon was the main language spoken, though in remoter areas some would probably have hung onto Celtic and a few would have picked up the Vikings' Norse. Birdlip is thought to be a corruption of the name of some Viking warrior, and as for Elcombe itself, 'combe' is Old English for a small valley in the side of a hill, but may well be of Celtic origin. The 'El' could conceivably come from similar words in Old English and Norse meaning 'bend' or 'elbow', but I am not aware of any definitive etymology. The lane coming down from Swifts Hill certainly does make an 'elbow' at the combe.

Next came the Normans – and William the Conqueror promptly dispossessed most English landowners in Gloucestershire in order to reward his nobles and followers, while of course keeping something for himself. The Domesday census in 1086 showed the king owning nearly 20 per cent of the county. The first written mention of Gloucestershire as a shire had occurred in a document a few years earlier – 1016. Our mother village of Bisley was by then well enough established to be recorded in the Domesday Book. Counties were divided into administrative regions called Hundreds (originally believed to have embraced a hundred families) and the Bisley Hundred included Stroud, Painswick and several surrounding villages.

One of the beneficiaries of King William's largesse was the family of Roger de Mortimer and his son Ralph, who had been among his chief army commanders both before and during the conquest. They received a portion of the Manor of Bisley — evidently including Elcombe, as we shall see — and held it for the best part of two centuries until a dissident descendant — another Roger Mortimer — was executed for treason in 1330. Even then, the family got their land back not long afterwards.

The 12th century was marked by widespread anarchy and famine as competing Norman factions fought for supremacy, in Gloucestershire as elsewhere. Many barons took to pillage and torture — the poor, as usual, being the ones to suffer most.

2 THE FIRST 700 YEARS
1200-1900 AD

The first resident of Elcombe known by name was a certain Anis Stanton, who had "one grange called Elcombe" on a lease from landowner Roger Mortimer for an unknown period upto 1357. A grange was a farmhouse or granary, and with it came four 'lands' (fields). Stanton was presumably a member of one of the oldest Bisley families, which is still represented in the area today. We only know about him because he is mentioned as the previous occupant in a document of 1357 granting to William Sered "one grange called Elcombe to be held of him and his heirs for 4s. [four shillings] per annum".

The lease was granted by 'the court of Roger Mortimer', apparently the latest scion of the dynasty, unless the court overseeing the Mortimer estates retained the name of an earlier Roger. That would surely not have been his most immediate eponymous forbear, who had taken King Edward II's wife, Isabella, as his lover and virtually ruled England for three years after contriving the King's murder. The Mortimer lands were confiscated by the Crown for some years after that Roger was arrested, tried and hanged in 1330.

The ecclesiastical records of Worcester Diocese show that a few years earlier, in March 1348, a priest by the name of Edmund de Elcomb was appointed Perpetual Vicar of the Church of Byslee. This was only 33 years after the High Altar of the church was consecrated and the construction of the chancel completed. The Bisley historian Mary Rudd suggests that Edmund may have been a member of the Sered family, but in fact perpetuity was rather short-lived in his case and he had resigned the vicarage in 1355, two years before Sered acquired the Elcombe lease (unless the 1357 document was a renewal of an existing lease). So maybe Edmund was one of the Stantons, or of a family

[11]

who were there before them. It's not unreasonable to guess that the first permanent settlement at Elcombe could have been 100 years earlier, bearing in mind that there was already a mill operating at the neighbouring hamlet of The Vatch in 1287.

On his appointment, Edmund had been presented to the Bishop by the Rector of Bisley, Richard de Clavill. But de Clavill's successor, Peter de Lacey, asked to be relieved of the care of souls. The question went to a formal inquiry and Edmund's resignation, one must assume, was prompted by their finding that the care of souls was his job, not the Rector's. Perhaps the idea of trudging two miles up the hill every day was too much for him. Judging by his colleagues, churchmen of the day favoured Norman name forms with the possessive 'de', and Edmund followed suit, so that we know where he was from without knowing his family.

Also in the 1350s, the court of Bisley Manor appointed three woodwards – officials responsible for the management of woodlands – for the areas of Bussage, Oakridge and Wygesty. Since no one today seems to recognise a wood with the old Saxon name of Wygesty, the Victoria History of Gloucestershire helpfully notes that it was "sometimes alternatively known as the woodward of Timbercombe or Catswood".

Turn again, Whittington!

Between Elcombe and Bisley lies Lypiatt Park, an ancient estate which, the old-timers used to say, once owned Elcombe and rented the cottages to its farm workers. In Edmund de Elcomb's time, Lypiatt Park was sold by Alexander of Duntisbourne to William Mansell, who already owned land around Bisley (Frampton Mansell?). But Mansell's son, Philip, defaulted on a loan of £500 from Richard Whittington, a wealthy mercer, who thus acquired it on Philip's death in 1396. Mansell could at least console himself that he was in good company as a mortgagee of Whittington: others accepting loans from him included Richard II, Henry IV and Henry V. The following year, 1397, presumably after his legendary walk to the capital with his cat, Dick Whittington was elected Lord Mayor of London – and he was re-elected twice after that, in 1406 and 1419. If Roger Mortimer had wanted to sell the freehold of Elcombe, Dick Whittington would surely have had the resources to buy it from him.

A descendant of Dick Whittington was still at Lypiatt in 1491.

Eighty years later, after it had changed hands, the estate owned 50 houses, 10 mills and some 4,400 acres of land. These holdings were extended even further by Thomas Stephens and his family in the 1600s. Meanwhile, Bisley was prospering: tax assessments show that in 1574 the village paid 13 times as much on its income as it had two centuries earlier – more even than Cirencester.

The Mortimer estates (still including Elcombe, as far as we know) were handed down through several more generations before passing by marriage to Richard, Duke of York. Unlike other landowners, Richard was said to be casual about raising rents or even obtaining payment of those due. This was perhaps because he was more interested in pursuing his claim to the throne, and because he needed the political support of his estate managers and those under them. When Richard died in 1460 at the Battle of Wakefield, Bisley Manor reverted to the Crown. In 1608, King James I granted the manor to the Marquis of Buckingham, after whom it passed through two other hands before eventually being bought by the aforementioned Thomas Stephens of Lypiatt.

And so we see that Elcombe did indeed become part of the Lypiatt estate. At this time, around 1700, Bisley parish had about 3,200 inhabitants, living in 710 houses – which, at an average of 4.5 people per house, does not suggest any serious problem of overcrowding. But few could think of buying their houses: only 103 were lucky or scheming enough to own their homes freehold.

After the 14th century records of Stanton, Sered and Edmund, there seems to be a gap of 300 years before anything else of significance was reported in the vicinity of Elcombe. Then came the civil war, and at the beginning of August 1643 King Charles I was leading his army westward to the siege of Gloucester. On the 8th of that month, the army came down from Lypiatt – first across fields and then down through the steep, wooded hill above the hamlet. They would have passed what is now the hairpin bend before continuing down the rough, green-canopied lane. With enemy troops in the valley below,

---

Overleaf: The oldest surviving property deed is for the sale of Elcombe Cottages "made the Twenty Sixth Day of December in the Tenth Year of the reign of our Sovereign Lord George the Third...", that is, 1769. The purchaser, William Jennings, Baker, acquired the semi-detached pair of cottages from Jane Viner, widow of a joiner, for the sum of £21. Both cottages had tenants, so they were evidently seen as a rental investment

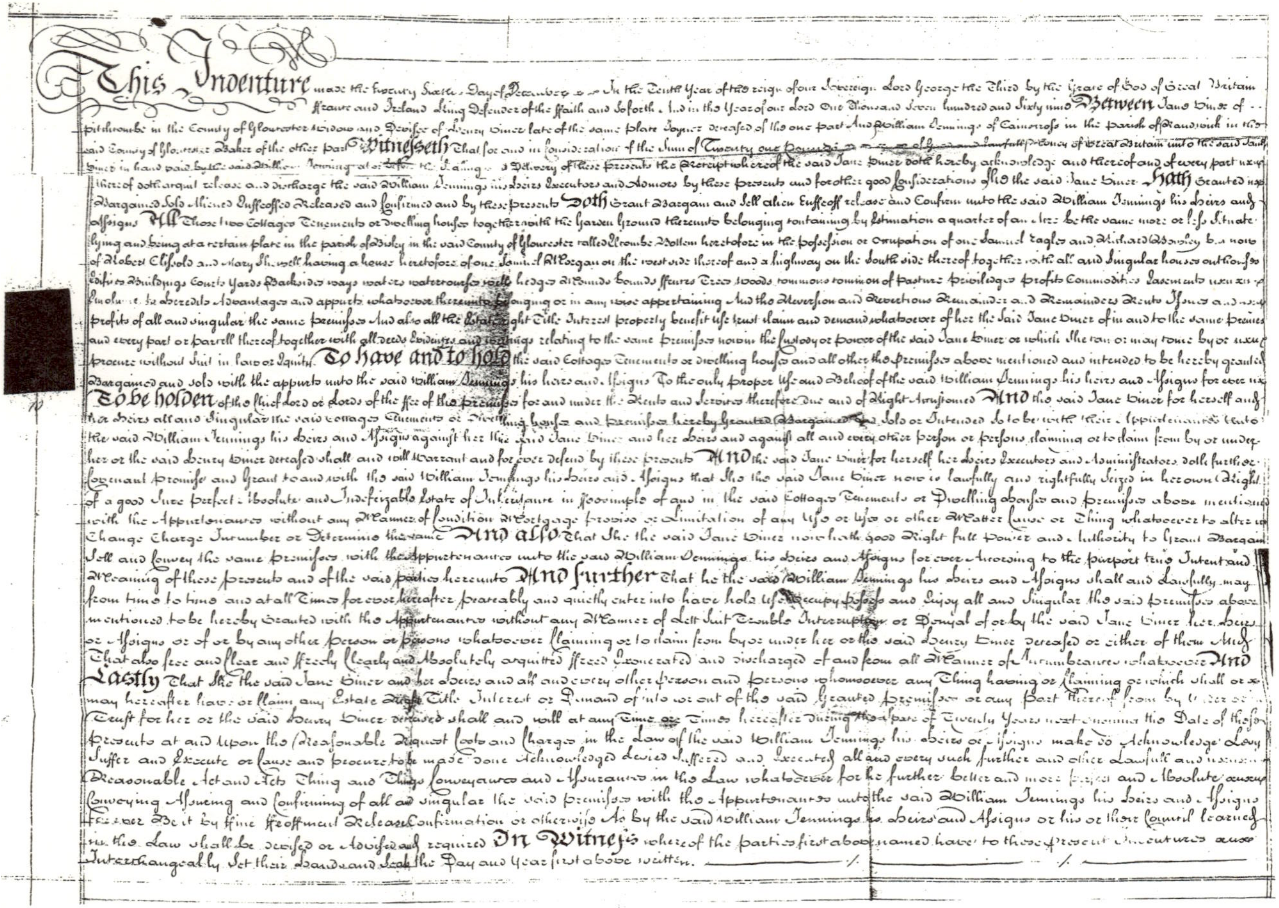

they evidently chose this route to keep out of sight. And they managed it because – as Professor R.H. Tawney (Rose Cottage) describes it in one of his books, "some enterprising staff officer contrived – heaven knows how – to get the army down it on its way to the siege..."

By this time there were probably some other houses at Elcombe. The original part of Furner's Farm is reckoned to be 16th century, though partly rebuilt and extended in the 17th and again in the late 19th. A former owner of Springfield Cottage, Ron Lanchbury, always maintained that his house dated from 1650, though any evidence for this is not known to the present writer. Certainly from this time until the end of the 18th century there must have been an increasing demand for labour in the Slad Valley with several mills already in operation, and the associated need for housing was quite possibly what prompted a building boom at Elcombe. According to the Victoria History, "the establishment of a group of cottages...at Elcombe on the boundary with Stroud had begun by 1734". Many of the cottages do appear to have 18th century origins, though, as we shall see later, almost all of them have undergone extensive remodelling by their infinitely more prosperous owners of the 20th. What remains unclear

Riches of history on our doorstep

Social history can be approached by several paths, Professor Tawney declared in a lecture to the National Book League in 1949*. One such path would start from a familiar scene of daily life – and England, like most of her European neighbours, was a country where "something amusing or tragic has occurred at every corner". And without mentioning it by name, he took Elcombe as an example.

"A tump – what the cultured call a tumulus – with neolithic bones which the aged roadman at last consented not to throw away; a precipitate lane beside it, known to the natives, though not to writers of guide-books, as King Charles' Hill, because, on an early day in August 1643 some enterprising staff officer contrived – Heaven knows how – to get the army down it on its way to the siege of the godly city the unforeseen tenacity of whose obstinate shopkeepers wrecked the year's campaign; twenty minutes one way the room in which, forty years before, the Catholic Throckmorton of the day had brooded with Catesby over projects for the famous plot [to overthrow Queen Elizabeth I]; twenty minutes

the other the farm called Abbey Farm, seized, two generations earlier, by the Defender of the Faith from a local religious house; a mile north the high point known as Wittentree Clump, where the wise men of the district are thought to have assembled in Saxon times and the Home Guard met in our own; a mile east a village not finally enclosed till the sixties of the last century, in circumstances some of which — characteristically, the Comic, not the sad — twenty years ago old men still recounted; a mile south the magnificent wrought-iron gates of the Haunted House, the work — so the probably mendacious story runs — of a smith convicted for murder, whom a wicked judge consented to spare, on condition that he made them, and then, when they were made, proceeded to hang; in the distance the hill from which, Mr Madden** has told us, Clement Perks of the Hill, in Henry IV, took his designation, with the hamlet at its foot inhabited by the 'arrant knave' favoured by Mr Justice Shallow, the name of which is pronounced in the improbable manner in which Shakespeare, who, to judge by his spelling, must have heard it spoken, decided to write it — all, except the last, demand no more than tolerable boots and a longish afternoon.

"These human associations are as vital and moving a part of the landscape as its hills and streams. There are many districts, urban not less than rural, as rich or richer in them. If education does not use them, of what use are they? I have never taught children; so, like everyone else in that position, I know exactly how to do it. A one-inch ordnance survey map as the teacher's bible; an attempt to lead the older of the little victims to see and feel scenes every day beneath their eyes; a few good books, when such exist, in which to read of what they saw; and only then a gradual advance towards wider horizons — such would be some of the ingredients in my prescription."

There is a lot of history on our doorstep — but I wonder how many of us who have called Elcombe home can readily identify even the few places that Tawney mentions as part of that heritage? Throckmorton, I've since learned, was the owner of Lypiatt Park in the late 16th century; Abbey Farm is at The Vatch; Wittentree at the highest point on this part of the escarpment, near Stancombe; Bisley the village lately enclosed, and Nether Lypiatt Manor the haunted one.

---

* Published posthumously as one of the essays and articles in The Radical Tradition, George Allen & Unwin, 1964. ** D H Madden had identified 'the hill' with Stinchcombe, while the hamlet Woodmancote (Woncot) is now part of Dursley.

is when the Elcombe cottages – or land – were sold off by Lypiatt; by the late 1700s, in any event, at least one and possibly all of them were independently owned.

The 17th and early 18th centuries were generally a prosperous time for the Cotswolds, but most landowners and mill bosses were disinclined to share their increasing wealth with the workers who made it possible. One gentleman of the time is on record as declaring: "Everyone knows that the lower classes must be kept poor or they will never be industrious". Often a labourer's wages were not enough to buy bread for his family, let alone other necessities. This led to mounting protests by farm workers early in the 19th century, which the government stifled by banning unauthorised demonstrations. But another wave of revolt swept the countryside in the 1870s over low pay and long working hours.

Turning towards Stroud
Although there had been a rough lane into Stroud for some time earlier, it was probably only after 1800 – when the new Cheltenham-Bath road was built up the valley – that Stroud began to supersede Bisley as Elcombe's gateway to the outside world. Already 20 years earlier Stroud had got a canal link to the River Severn, making it the business hub of the district; the London road along the Golden Valley (1814) added to the town's prosperity, and this was consolidated with the advent of the railway in 1845.

By the 19th century, the mill economy was on the wane and before the end of the century Vatch Mill was the only one left in Slad. The common land of Dunkite Hill on the north side of Elcombe was privatised by the enclosures of the 1860s, which led to violent protests elsewhere in Bisley. Dunkite Hill was sold off as two large parcels and six smaller ones. The largest, of 10 acres and 5 perches, was approximately the area now attached to Under Catswood and it sold for £115. It was bought by a Stroud solicitor, but it appears he was acting for (or later sold to) Dorrington of Lypiatt. This assignment stipulated that "the fences on every side where abutting against old inclosures are to be made and for ever hereafter maintained and repaired by the owner of such piece and parcel of land." The second largest, being 2 acres, 3 rods and 7 perches, was roughly the area now belonging partly to Rose Cottage and partly to its former owner, John Papworth.

John Edward Dorrington of Lypiatt bought a smaller lot bordering the hairpin bend and King Charles' Lane. Of four small plots bordering the lane where Rose Cottage and Hillside now stand, one was bought by Thomas Lewis and the other by John Bartlett, both of Elcombe.

The 1851 Census

The first detailed information on residents of Elcombe comes from the 1851 census. It records eight households and two unoccupied properties – a total of 10, compared with the 13 in the year 2000 (or 14 including Fletcher's Knapp's converted pigsties, made habitable and tenanted since the late 1990s). The difference is partly accounted for by Under Catswood, which was built much later, and Furner's Farm Cottage, which was an outbuilding not a habitable dwelling in 1851. That leaves one house not listed in the census – possibly Fletcher's Knapp, which then (in its original form) belonged to Furner's Farm and may have started life as a barn.

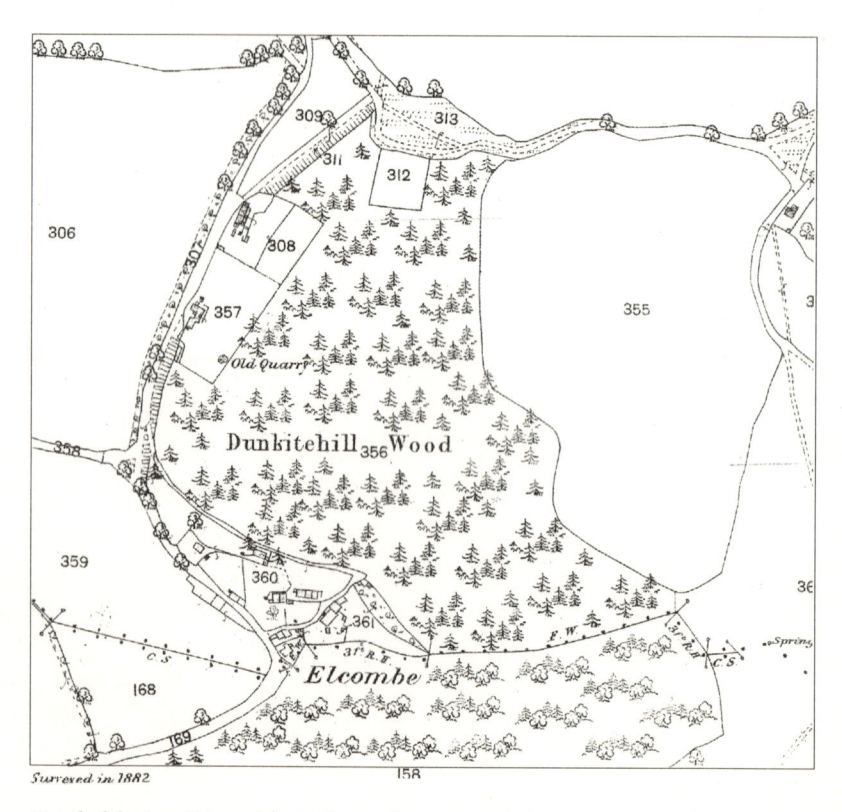

Detail of the 1st edition of the Ordnance Survey map, 1884

Apart from Furners Farm, all the householders listed in the census were described as agricultural labourers. Since the cottages did not have names, we cannot be sure where all of them lived, but in one of the Elcombe Cottages there was George King, his wife Lucy and sister Emily; in the other, Thomas and Hannah Snow, both pensioners, though she was still listed as 'agricultural labourer' at the age of 77. At Yew Tree Cottage were Daniel and Sophia Selwyn, while at Furners Farm was the widowed Sarah Mayo with four children aged 13 to 26 and a servant. Other households were those of Eli and Comfort Davies, with three young sons and a daughter; widower Jas Tyrell, with a son, daughter and nephew; and Thomas and Hannah King, plus two sons and a daughter, all in their 20s. The great majority of these residents were born within the parish of Bisley, a few having come across the valley from Painswick. Only one or two, out of a total of 38, were born further afield.

Just four years earlier, the John Edward Dorrington mentioned above had bought Lypiatt Park with 230 acres. He was a wealthy Londoner, being Clerk of the Fees and Chief Clerk of the Public Bills at the House of Commons, and he determined to restore the shrunken estate to its former glory. Over the previous century it had changed hands several times and many farms had been sold to pay accumulating debts. But in just 27 years before his death in 1874, Dorrington bought nine farms, including Catswood, expanding the estate again to 3,000 acres. His son, also John Edward, determined to enclose the 900 acres of Bisley Common. Many of the poor, who grazed their animals on the common, opposed the scheme, but its proponents argued it would make the land more productive, avoid diseases being spread by straying animals and give the parish much more income. Of course, they won, but not without incurring some civil resistance and a lot of public resentment. Stone walls that Dorrington had built on the new boundaries were knocked down, and a crowd stoned two policemen who were hiding in the hope of catching the perpetrators. Though there is no record of any riots in Elcombe over the enclosure of Dunkite Hill, it's hard to imagine that the people of the hamlet were not vehemently opposed to this land grab. After this, the people of Stroud refused to elect Dorrington as their MP.

Through the 19th century, farming in this part of the Cotswolds was predominantly of sheep and corn. Wool from the sheep had been the cornerstone of the area's prosperity for two or three centuries, providing the raw material for dozens of mills strung out along the five valleys radiating from Stroud. But apart from the country squires in their manor houses, some farmers and the most prosperous tradesmen, few people could afford to own their own homes.

Yew Tree Cottage is a case in point. Up to 1827 it was owned by a Thomas Whiting – probably a scion of the large Bisley family of that name – and a John Whiting owned the house next door, Hillside. One may assume that neither of them actually lived there: this was buy-for-rent 19th century style. And when Thomas Whiting sold for £15, the purchaser was Rachel Gregory "of Ferners", who rented it out or used it as a tied cottage for one of her farm workers. From then until the end of the century, Yew Tree had four owners and a succession of tenants. When sold in 1896, its value had gone up to £50 – an increase of 330% in 70 years, compared with 1,100% in 20 years a century later.

So the people who *owned* the houses at Elcombe were probably moderately prosperous, having their own jobs in Bisley or elsewhere and a bit of rent as well. The people who actually *lived* here were probably among the poorest of the rural poor.

The pub and the brothel

One of the stories that keeps circulating despite a lack of known proof is that at some time in the past Elcombe had its own public house. It is true that between 1769 and 1806 two residents – Joseph and John Clissold of Elcombe Cottages – were listed as 'innholders', and publicans most often lived on the premises. It's also true that it would have been a hard trudge to Slad or Bisley for farmworkers to get a drink at the end of a long day's work. But if there were an ale house, it would have to have been something much more modest than The Bear or most of the dozen other pubs then registered at Bisley; probably just a small, smoky room in one of those two cottages, possibly with a bit of a terrace outside for the summer.

Another story – improbable as it may sound now – says that for farm workers with any energy left at the end of the day there was also a brothel in the middle of fields at the Scrubs, a mile or so up the valley. According to a reliable source from an old farming family, this house of ill repute shared a small stone building with a shop. Anyway, both businesses must have suffered a recession a long time ago. All that is left, this informant says, are some ruins of the building.

Crime and violence

One can imagine that when serious fighting or other crimes occurred in Elcombe, the offenders would be marched up the hill to Bisley and clamped into the lock-up. The two draughty cells are still there today, just a few yards from The Bear Inn. The lock-up was built or rebuilt in 1824 to hold prisoners temporarily until the Law decided their fate. And what sort of crimes might the miscreants have committed? Well, perhaps facing hunger or just wanting a good meal for his family, it would have been tempting for a poor labourer to kidnap the odd sheep from a farmer's field. Indeed, in 1646 in Bisley a notice was issued:

> "To the constables, tythingmen and other of the King's Majestie's officers within the parish of Bisley...Forasmuch as I am informed by Willm Hancocks that he hath had divers sheepe feloniously taken from him and that he hath in suspicion divers persons dwelling in ye said Parish – These are therefore to authorise you...to make diligent search...and to apprehend all suspected persons...and thereupon to bring them before me or some other of the King's Ma'ties Justices of the Peace. Fayle you not at yor perill."

Of other crimes or acts of violence in Elcombe we have no information until the 20th century, when one or more of its people spent time in police stations or prisons – though in John Papworth's case (Chapter 8) for what most would consider honourable dissent. (Papworth himself recalls being threatened by a gun-toting farmer for alleged trespass higher up the valley.) In the 1930s, when he 'went a bit queer', Old Will King chased people with an axe, and the same kind of weapon, wielded by Elcombe's man-in-the-woods Gerry Vaughan, featured in the 1990s saga over the fence around the spring (Chapter 11). In the context of family feuds, no one was charged over the brutal nighttime attack on Reg Bartlett on Swifts Hill, from which it is said he never fully recovered, dying at the age of 43. Prosperity – with a television in every home – has brought the odd burglary from time to time, but nothing more serious. As for poaching, there's evidence that it still continues, albeit on a small scale. In recent years, there would occasionally be unidentified cars parked at night on the lane under Tranters Hill and from the cottage terraces one would see furtive flashes of a torch in the woods where there are no paths and hear one man calling to another in the dark. On one occasion, Gwen Wenman saw two men with guns standing close to her cottage. All in all, however, Elcombe can still consider itself a quiet and peaceful place.

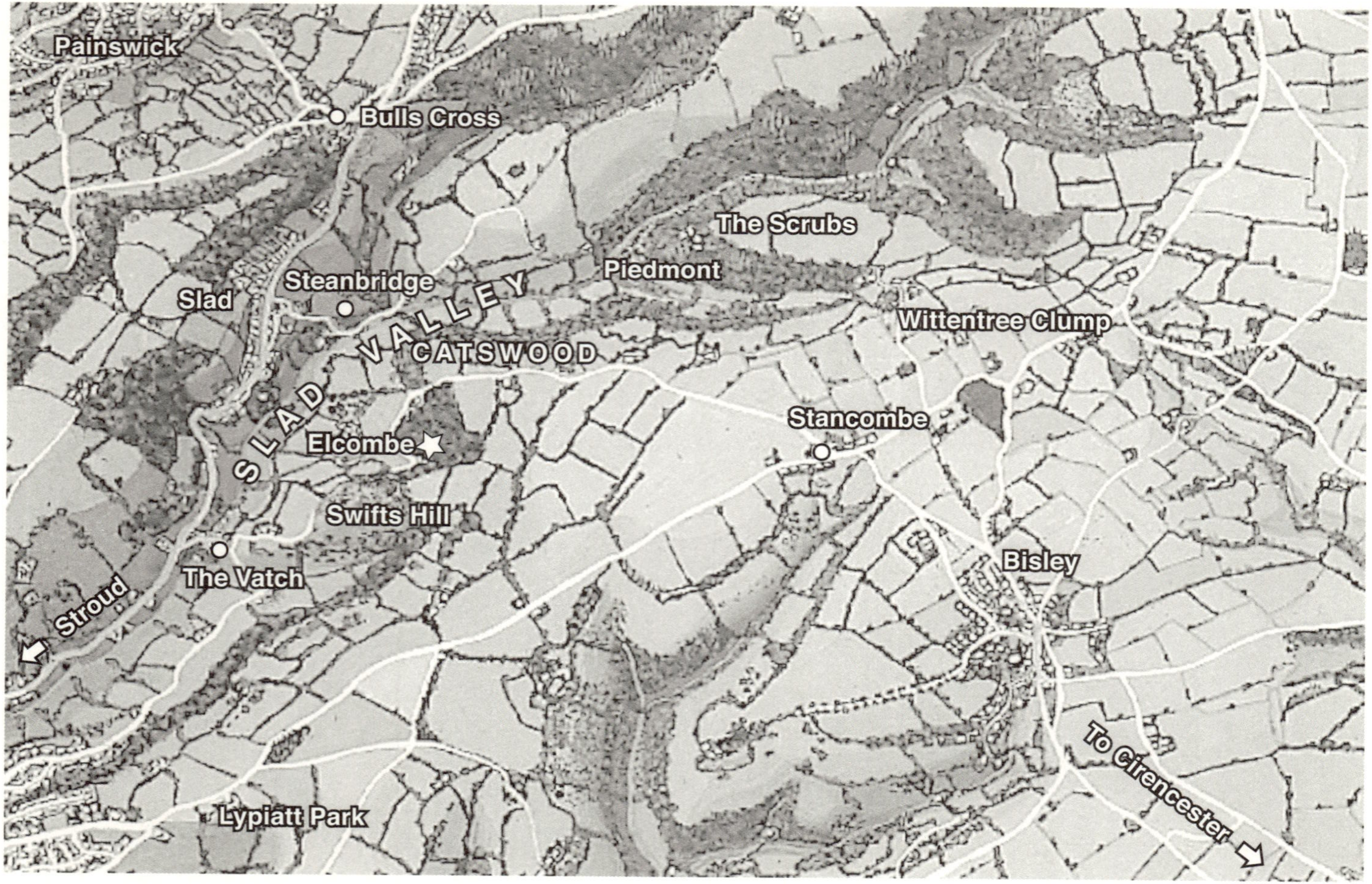

MAP ARTWORK COURTESY OF RICHARD CHANDLER

3 DRAMATIC TRANSFORMATIONS
The 20th Century

Life in Elcombe just 100 years ago was almost unimaginably different from that of its residents today. There are the obvious things: no electricity, no tap water or flush toilets, no telephones or television, not even radio broadcasting – and no transport faster than a horse and cart. (It's unlikely that many penny-farthings made it up the hill from The Vatch). On the other hand, some things worked better then. In April 1902, the Stroud News reported: "The ever-progressive Slad people have recently had greater postal facilities granted them. They are now able to post a letter at nine o'clock in the morning and receive a reply the same day."

Apart from the material differences, there are also the things one can't measure: what it meant to walk to Stroud and back every day for work, rain or shine; the church-going and the communal entertainments; and the fact of everyone 'knowing their place' in the social order, which was a device for keeping most of them in penury.

But change was not long in coming. In the first decade of the century, the rural economy of the Cotswolds, which had for a long time been centred on sheep and corn, fell victim to imports of grain, wool and meat from overseas. The result: a major shift to dairy cattle in the 1920s. By this time, too, both of Bisley's big land-owning estates had been broken up. After Lypiatt, it was the turn in 1919 of the Bisley Estate, who were landlords to most other tenant farmers of the district. This estate had been in the hands of Arthur Stanton, a scion of the old Bisley family associated with the earliest references to Elcombe in the 14th century.

At this time, however, Elcombe had already ceased to be a community of agricultural workers and had become one of tradesmen, factory workers and the like – their employment causing them to

[23]

Children of Slad School, just after World War I. Bill Fern of Yew Tree Cottage, in cap and overcoat, stands far left, and his older sister Gwen, with long hair over her shoulders, beside the teacher. Two of their cousins, Sybil and Martin Fern, are at the back, far right

gravitate more and more to Stroud. There was a shoemaker at Rose Cottage, who had his own shop in town; a mechanic, a postman, a brewery worker, a stone mason. Apart from the owners of Furners Farm, it seems that only one family – the Bartletts of Springfield Cottage – worked on the land.

Another revolution

This profile of occupations had changed again dramatically by the end of the century. In the mid-1990s there was still one cowman (soon to be gone), but the others were: two artists (one a baronet), retired fireman, retired lawyer, two vets, woodcarver and gilder, journalist, architect's widow, two retired theatrical agents, businessman and teacher – overwhelmingly representatives of the educated and prosperous middle class. This reflects a revolution that Elcombe has shared with many Cotswold villages, but its causes and consequences are worth examining.

In 1769, the price of a one-up, one-down cottage in Elcombe was about £10. By 1830 it had risen to £15-25. Around 1900, one cottage sold for £100 – probably about the average at the start of the 20th century. By the 1930s, our humble abodes were fetching around £300 and 20 years later, after World War II, perhaps £500. In 1964 – now with mains electricity and running water, which had arrived in the hamlet just 10 years earlier – Yew Tree Cottage (three-up, three-down at this time) changed hands for £1,400. Over the next 12 years its market value rocketed by 1400% and it was sold in 1976 for £20,000. But that was only the start of the century's property price spiral: 22 years later the same house (well, not quite the same house, given some extension and remodelling in the meantime) sold for £235,000.

Scarcity value
The economist Fred Hirsch helped to explain this phenomenon in his book, *Social Limits to Growth* (Routledge & Kegan Paul, 1977). As he pointed out, the desirability of country cottages to an increasingly prosperous (and mobile) society could only mean steep increases in their value, since the stock was fixed. With the exception of the illustrious Professor Tawney, who acquired Rose Cottage in 1928, the middle-class invasion of this rural backwater began in World War II with at least two city-dwellers seeking a safe haven from air raids. But they needed to be hardy, given the absence of public utilities and the need to carry water from the spring with buckets on a yoke. In the 1950s and '60s came three or four more and by the 1970s the takeover was virtually complete.

The consequences of this social transformation have been profound. Upto the 1950s, several of the old residents were people born in the valley, if not in Elcombe itself, and they spoke a dialect that would sometimes be difficult to understand for incomers brought up on a homogenised English. Nowadays, no one is a Slad native and the ancient dialect is dead. In this sense, Elcombe is a microcosm of the universal process of globalisation, with its cultural standardisation and economic extortion. Everywhere, in Elcombe or in El Paso, indigenous people have been exploited to the point that they can no longer afford what should have been their birthright: a place to live in their own community. Many locals who would have liked these cottages have been priced out of the market. The supremacy of the power of money over human need and social justice is the hallmark of the 'free market economy' that we still seem happy to say our prayers to. At the same time, it must be recognised that many people born and brought up in the countryside found that with the demise of the rural economy and their place in it, a modern housing estate in or near the town suited their new television/fast food/car-based lifestyle better than the typical cramped cottage. Not surprisingly, those old enough to remember the rural life as one of hardship and poverty were glad to leave it behind, and many were able to afford a more spacious home and modern conveniences with the price that tired city-dwellers were ready to pay them. The snag is that, apart from the few who may be able to move speedily up the economic ladder, once departed from the village they are never able to go back. The disparity between the price of country cottages (desired by the well-heeled middle class) and urban semis continues to widen, almost by the month.

The end of self-sufficiency
In the 1920s, the wives of Elcombe collected their bread three times a week from the Star and carried it home in bolsters. "Quatern loaves they were", recalled Gwen Fern.* At that time, milk cost 1½d a quart (equivalent to three pints for 1p in today's money) and they could also get buttermilk, which Gwen said was very good for rice puddings. Coal for cooking and heating was delivered by horse and cart and cost £1 a ton.

Upto the end of World War II, which was perhaps the biggest watershed in the transformation of village life, the villagers of Elcombe were able to maintain a balanced diet with a high degree of self-sufficiency. Gardens were used primarily for growing vegetables rather than flowers, and for their protein they could depend largely on their homegrown chickens and pigs, combined with a selection of game such as rabbit, rook pie (not much featured by our TV chefs these days!) and doubtless some poached pheasant or lamb when they could get it. The remains of old pigsties can still be seen in some gardens – in one case now occupied by humans.

But then, with the end of the war, the government outlawed the slaughtering of pigs on private premises, effectively banning them from garden sties. This marked the end of food self-sufficiency and the first step towards what would become, within a few decades, almost total dependency on supermarkets. Agriculture was also mechanising and all but the poorest farms in the area had traded in their plough-horses for tractors.

---

* A quatern loaf was a 4lb loaf, made from a quarter of a stone of flour.

Arthur Sam Bartlett, pictured on The Pitch with one of his sows and a healthy litter

Modernisation – from electric light to agrichemicals – has wrought many changes on the natural world of the Slad Valley. From her memories of childhood in the aftermath of World War I, Gwen Fern's recollection of decorating her hat with a ribbon of glowworms is not one that could be repeated by any Elcombe children today. Glowworm numbers all over the country have been decimated, partly by loss of their grassland habitat (not such a problem around Elcombe, one might think) but also by the ubiquity of electric lights, which confuse the males looking for a luminous partner.

Cuckoo flowers and water bubbles

In Gwen Fern's time, the fields around Elcombe were adorned with cuckoo flowers and water bubbles. The first of these were long-stemmed, little blue-mauve flowers that grew on the edge of ponds, while water bubbles were big yellow flowers with large leaves. And there were nightjars and nightingales. Much later, in the 1980s, nuthatches raised their young in a nesting box at Yew Tree Cottage, but after a few years they were never seen again.

Summing up her memories, Gwen said: "Time seemed to stand still then – we were very happy".

People are inclined to blame the wireless, or the advent of mains water, or the car, for spelling the end of the traditions of community in village life. In reality it was all of these and, perhaps most important, the sociological changes mentioned above which accompanied them. With the wireless, people spent less time in each other's houses

Gwen Fern of Yew Tree Cottage, and her half-sister Dorothy, 1937

during long winter evenings; with mains water, you didn't meet your neighbours at the spring; and with a car you could choose your friends in a wide radius, not just along the lane – and it insulated you from sharing transport with anyone else.

Special occasions
In the early era of the wireless, the 1920s, there were still concerts or dances every week or fortnight at the Timber Hut in Slad, and almost everyone from Elcombe would go, children and adults together. For the children, there was also an Annual Outing from Slad. In the old days, the transport for this consisted of two horses pulling a big hay waggon and everyone took sandwiches and drinks for a picnic. Later, the horses gave way to a charabanc (motor coach).

Naturally, holidays were special. At Christmas, several families in Elcombe benefited from the Bisley Calico Bequest – a charity which provided the poor of the parish with three yards of cloth or sometimes a half-hundredweight of coal. (At the coal price mentioned above, that would be 6d worth - 2½p in today's money – but it might at least have kept them warm from Christmas until New Year's Day.)

Easter was one occasion when quite a lot of people used to walk up through Elcombe on their way to Good Friday Tea at a small, non-conformist chapel. Higher up the valley, this chapel was apparently known as the Scrubs' Cathedral. They held a service in the afternoon, after which tea was served on the lawn outside with home-made bread and cakes and milk from one of the farms. Then there was an evening service, after which – one account relates – "everyone walked home by moonlight".

Flora and fauna

The hillsides around Elcombe are rich in wildlife, even though some garden birds and other creatures have seriously declined in numbers in recent decades due to loss of habitat, poisoning by agrichemicals or other causes. Among the noticeable (or audible) denizens of the surrounding woods are the Little Owls, whose hoots echo hauntingly across the stillness of the valley at night, and the badgers, who have their setts in many banks and are frequently caught in car headlights as they shuffle along the lanes. The badgers aim to deter anyone

'Above Elcombe, October' - oil on board, Oliver Heywood

from having pretensions of an elegant lawn, coming along to dig it up at regular intervals in search of some tasty morsel, not to mention the tulip bulbs they fancy. There is also a variable population of pheasants, squirrels, foxes, rabbits, stoats and weasels.

But the particular wealth of wildlife is on Swifts Hill, which boasts at least 11 species of orchid, as well as cowslip, columbine, harebell, yellow-wort, autumn gentian and viper's bugloss. Attracted by these flowers, 29 species of butterfly have been recorded here, including the Small Blue, Green Hairstreak, Dingy Skipper and the Duke of Burgundy's Fritillary (which feeds on the cowslips).

The chronicler of the valley's wildlife in the latter years of the 20th century was Pat Cooper, Warden of the Elliott Nature Reserve, which is owned by the Gloucestershire Trust for Nature Conservation and known as Swifts Hill. Pat, who lives at The Rifleman's, is also an accomplished illustrator and has contributed regular articles and drawings to the local newsletter, Slad Valley News, since it was started in 1980. In an early issue, she extolled the delights of autumn:

> "The Reserve is putting on its winter garb of soft, sandy velvet, which can be viewed from The Slad, but don't let this fool anyone: amongst the withered grass and fallen leaves lies a treasure of shapes and colours to be marveled at, which changes at an alarming speed, a race of Nature's own to see what can be achieved before Winter puts the final flag down.
>
> "Rounded shapes and blobs appear on dead wood amongst yellowing grass and push up between fallen leaves. To be found are white toadstools – Tricholoma Columbetta – tucked beside the roadway on the Elcombe side, with false morels – Helvella. Further up the slopes large glistening domes push up and spread into patches of Boletus. Beautiful mauve Blewits cling together in patches, and, if you are lucky, a clump of Parasol mushrooms can be seen. Dancing among the higher pasture, in fragile buffs and greys, are specimens of the Psathyrella family."

Swifts Hill's wild flowers include many of Gloucestershire's rarer plants. Towards autumn, one may find the Broad Helleborine orchid, Carline Thistle, Meadow Cranesbill, Greater Knapweed – the last of these, as Pat Cooper tells us, containing "a miniature, teeming world of lurking crab spiders, day-flying moths, colourful weevils (beetles) and alive with flies, bees and bugs of all sorts." Then there is the Field Scabious and the tiny Milkwort. At other times one can find "the blues and whites of bugloss, speedwell and bluebells, punctuated with clumps of stitchwort...and cuckoo pint."

Elcombe from Tranters Hill in the 1930s - a scene still unmistakeable for anyone arriving in the hamlet today

Apart from such occasions, Elcombe has never had many casual visitors. Most non-residents these days are those who stop short at Swift's Hill to walk their dogs and admire the breathtaking view from the top all the way to the Severn Bridge.

To celebrate the end of World War I, all the residents of Slad, The Vatch and Elcombe were invited to a tea party by the local squire at Steanbridge House. Gwen Fern remembers: "We [children] were all in fancy dress. I was Queen and Jack Brown [of Hillside] was King. We joined Chalford Brass Band at the Star Inn and walked with them through Slad to Steanbridge. It was a lovely day, warm and sunny. We all enjoyed a delicious tea and entertainment on the lawn by the lake. On our departure we received an apple and an orange, and a good time was had by all."

For King Jack and Queen Gwen, who would not have recognised that tea party as the end of an era, it was certainly the start of one quite different from that of their parents.

Run-up to the millennium

Thirty-five years later, after the end of World War II, Britain was beginning to enjoy a long wave of never-had-it-so-good material prosperity, and the takeover of Elcombe by the middle-class and their bourgeois values was soon nearly complete. In 1958, bureaucrats with little respect for such things severed the hamlet's historic ties with Bisley, placing it instead in the redrawn administrative boundaries of Painswick.

By this time, life was a bit easier for the women of Elcombe. Though they still had to walk to The Vatch and back, they could now go shopping in Stroud using the buses that ran up and down the valley every two hours.

Seaside holidays – a rare luxury for rural folk and tradesmen before the war – were rapidly transformed from a bucket-and-spade outing to Weston-super-Mare to package tours in Spain, and from there to more exotic destinations. Before long, Elcombe was sending its envoys to Africa, Asia, the Americas – and no one thought anything of it. The Slad Valley News began to carry travel reports from people visiting such far-flung spots as the Okavango Delta (Botswana) and the Andaman Islands in the Indian Ocean.

At home, it was getting harder to mobilise people for any social purpose. Back in the 1960s, Elcombe had mounted (if that's the right word) quite a lively anti-hunting lobby, described by John Papworth in his 'Rural Notebook':

> 'I had never, until recently, seen a hunt at close quarters, but this is hunting country and when strangers sawed off a tree trunk blocking the entrance to the bit of wood behind [Rose] cottage, and when the same strangers took to blocking up the holes of the badger setts with not quite empty herbicide drums, we realised something was up and that a foxhunt was in the offing.
>
> 'The threat aroused the dormant sense of community in the hamlet and we discovered there was a 100% anti-hunting front among us. The evil-smelling drums were pulled out of the tunnel holes of the unfortunate badgers by two sisters whose lives are devoted to dog breeding; the retired doctor's wife [Marian Francis] – a lovely woman and one of the great classical cooks of our time – hurriedly tacked a large notice to a tree saying "Nature Reserve – Hunt keep out"; and a lady who is believed to run a theatrical agency in London [Josephine Stroud or Judith Craig] dragged some more branches across the wood entrance.
>
> 'Was it our prejudice that when the hunt arrived the men on their horses all looked so bossy and bilious, and that the women looked

such a hard-faced lot, like female traffic wardens on a day trip? I rather think not, especially as the girls, like their horses nervous and highly strung, were really rather fetching. Or is that more prejudice?

'They trailed along the lane and held earnest conferences with an important looking man in a red coat on the fox's whereabouts; actually we had seen the animal disappear into our wood, but we kept mum about this and made what the doctor's wife called 'non-violent noises' against hunting in general. Finally they descended into the valley along King Charles' Hill and spent a fruitless half-hour around a foxhole in a field on Fletcher's farm before dispersing..."

After that, no similar mobilisation occurred in Elcombe until the 1990s, which saw a full-scale furore over ownership of and access to the spring. This is recounted later in Chapter 11. In the meantime, people's local entertainments ranged from carboot sales and participating in the Woolpack quiz team to bell-ringing at Painswick church, eating out (indulgently) at places like the Country Elephant in Painswick or (more modestly) at one of the Indian restaurants in Stroud. And, of course, working in the ever-demanding gardens. Being perched, most of them, on the steep hillsides at an angle approaching 45 degrees, and terraced with drystone walls that collapsed like a trembling virgin at the first lascivious smile of Jack Frost, our gardens were fragile beauties in need of a constant chaperone.

Berry wine and blizzards

A few years after the advent of electricity, people found it difficult to recall the pitch blackness of Elcombe as it had been after

Steep gardens mean lots of terraces, using the lovely but frost-prone Cotswold stone

nightfall. Being able to switch it off with a flick, the new generation had little respect for the dark – and, with taps in every kitchen and bathroom, little understanding of the hardship all their forebears had endured to carry up drinking water in heavy buckets from the spring. Rather, the new upper-class peasants set to acquiring some rural culture by filling massed ranks of demijohns with boiled nettles or elderflower or redcurrants or vine leaves, and adding a pinch of yeast in the hope it would yield a drinkable 'country wine'. The author can say this since he was one of them. He can also say that the success rate was not high.

In the early 1980s there were as many as twelve children in Elcombe (though not all of them all the time) and about 22 resident or weekending adults. Even without harvests of glowworms, the children still had wonderful times, running free in the woods and fields, climbing trees, building hideouts and clambering over – or falling into – the Slad brook. Until the second half of that decade, winter nearly always brought some heavy snowfalls, giving the children lots of fun with toboganning and snowball fights. It wasn't unusual for Elcombe to be snowed up for several days, and an excursion on foot to The Bear at Bisley or the Stroud shops was liable to find you fighting your way home in a blizzard. But in recent years, everyone agrees, the climate has been changing and serious snowfalls seem to be less and less frequent. Winters are not what they used to be.

A typical wintry garden scene in the 1980s

4 THE LIE OF THE LAND
A walking tour

Across the fields and through the woods, there are several ways of approaching Elcombe by footpaths, some of them ancient rights of way. By the public highway – a single-track lane – the hamlet can be reached from its mother village of Bisley, higher up on the plateau, or from Stroud down in the valley. Being precipitous and twisting in places, as well as narrow, the lane attracts very little through traffic.

Starting from Stroud, there are two roads up the Slad Valley: either the main B4070 'Scenic Route', from which, after a couple of miles, there is a narrow turn-off signposted to The Vatch and Elcombe; or the old lane, which wends its way along the eastern slopes until swinging and dipping down to The Rifleman's and The Vatch. Between these two, a fork turns up the hill again, passing between the fine old Jacobean farmhouse of Knapp House on one side and its barns on the other. Then a steep climb to the base of Swifts Hill, passing the first of two cattle-grids installed in 1980 so that cows can be left to graze there without wandering off. The lane continues around the hill, rising further, until, near the second cattle-grid, one can pause at a field gateway for a splendid panorama of Slad and the whole valley. It is a vantage-point chosen by many photographers. In Susan Hill's book, *The Spirit of the Cotswolds,* this is the image she chooses to sum up that spirit. Of the Slad Valley in general, she says: "I know more spectacular bits of the Cotswolds, more famous, more obviously pretty, but I know nowhere that gives me such complete joy, that is quite so flawless, and yet real, living, not artificially preserved." On her last visit while preparing the book, she stood on this high, narrow road - "this magic spot" - and knew that she had found what she was looking for: "the place where the pure spirit of the Cotswolds bubbled out of the ground like a spring."

ALL ABOUT ELCOMBE

("Loik a spring of oipurrbole!" one of our old-timers might've commented, if they'd had the vocabulary for it.)

From here, the treeless hump of Swifts Hill gives way to the thickly-wooded Tranters Hill, underneath which the lane continues from the cattle-grid, downhill now for a quarter of a mile, until it reaches Elcombe.

On the Slad side, therefore, the history of our hamlet is intertwined with that of its neighbours, The Rifleman's and The Vatch (so named because its mill originally ground vetches), as well as with the farms of Knapp House and, further up the valley, Steanbridge. There was a Thomas Clissold owning the Vatch Mill in 1592, nearly 200 years before there are Clissolds recorded as living at Elcombe. The mill became one of a dozen in the valley, strung out from Stroud to Steanbridge and beyond. It grew to be five storeys high in the 19th century, with a ground area estimated at 35,000 sq ft or 175,000 sq ft in total – hard to imagine when one stands in the lane today.

The Vatch

In its heyday, Vatch Mill is reckoned to have had 600 workers, at least some of whom must have lived up the lane in Elcombe. And even if most of the other mills weren't half as big, twelve of them in the one valley meant a lot of industry. In 1825 there were riots when a large gathering of weavers tried to halt the practice of enforced overtime, whereby employees had to take a lot of work home. A number of people who opposed the protest were ducked in the Vatch millpond and the authorities sent a detachment of Hussars to arrest the ringleaders. By 1833, the mill was powered by three steam engines and two water-wheels. A few years later six power looms were added to the 55 handlooms, but only 50 years later the mill ceased production – and almost all the others in the valley had already closed. It had begun as a corn mill, became a fulling mill for the felting and cleansing of cloth

Vatch Mill, of which nothing now remains

by the early 1600s and a cloth mill in the Victorian era. The nearby Upper Vatch Mill – now the home of an antiquarian book business – was appropriately a paper mill.

The Vatch has until recently had some ripe characters of its own, not to mention a ghost. In one terrace of cottages – built from the bricks of the demolished mill – there was an old man, Hubert Twinning, whose cottage had been untouched in decoration or ornaments for 70 years. Believing his next-door neighbour to be spying on him with laser cameras, Twinning threatened to install a lead dividing wall. It was his father, Jack, who looked after Rose Cottage and garden for the Tawneys at Elcombe in the 1930s, and who one day had walked the several miles to Shurdington, his son recalled, to bring back Mrs Tawney's pony. Twinning's uncle, Lou Hanks, kept chickens on Tawney's paddock for a time.

Hanks had a reputation for being cantankerous, but John Papworth found him one of the most likeable men in the area. Living with his sister after returning from many years in Canada, Hanks invited Papworth to tea one Sunday. In his 'Rural Notebook', the latter remembered the meal as "a kind of monument to modern working-class culture. There was both white and brown bread, tinned salmon, boiled eggs, salad, currant cake, tinned fruit, cream and, of course, endless cups of strong tan-coloured tea."

In the same terrace as Hanks, there was also the ex-wife of a lord, and Dirty Doris, who was said to have been in charge of an intelligence centre in Stroud during World War II but in later years was reduced to the life of a bag lady. Doris was reputed to keep ducks in her bath – at least useful, since she never used it herself. The ghost – apparently seen by three different people in recent times – is said to inhabit Upper Vatch Mill, whose owner speculated that the house might have been a convent at some time. But the lady ghost was last seen wearing a long primrose dress with a high collar – hardly the prescribed attire for a nun.

The Rifleman's and Knapp House

The Rifleman's, another small group of cottages near The Vatch, is apparently so named because in the early 19th century local men were given musketry training in a nearby quarry amid fears of a Napoleonic invasion. When one of the houses later became a public house, it was named 'The Rifleman's Arms'.

On the knap or hillcrest immediately above the Vatch stands Knapp

Both Tranter's and Dunkite Hill had been pine plantations and both were clear-felled at the end of World War II, permitting this picture from a rarely available perspective

DAVID MYLES

House, said to date from the late 1600s. This fine old farmhouse of mellow stone belonged to the Webb family until they sold and moved to a more modest dwelling across the road, while keeping their land. With his herd of cows occupying the fields around, the father of the present generation was also the local milkman and became a local character still remembered today. No doubt in the tradition of outsized men who get nicknamed 'Tiny,' the generously-proportioned Farmer Webb became known as 'Boney'. And Boney Webb had a horse called Creamie, which turned his cider press as well as pulling the milk cart. According to one later Elcombe resident, Boney also had the reputation of being "a bit of a lad for watering his milk". One story that went the rounds was that when inspectors sprang out from a side road, Boney would crack the whip over Creamie so that the horse shot forward, the churns fell off the back of the cart and the spilt milk was untestable.

In his book *Ferns in the Valley*, Jim Fern, who was a schoolboy of Laurie Lee's generation, recalled that Boney Webb was "not known for his great affection for people who walked his fields, even though some of them were rights of way." He remembered him driving the milk cart,

> "a brown-smocked, non-smiling man standing on the step which protruded from the back of the float. With taut reins reaching out to the pony in front he looked like a charioteer of old. The pony, like those used by many others, was a lovely intelligent creature with the uncanny ability to find its way home if the farmer became over-tired or for some other reason."

The diplomatic Mr Fern means that after a stop at the pub, farmers – possibly not excepting Old Boney – were sometimes drunk and incapable, relying on this equine gift of navigation to get them back to the farm.

Swifts Hill

Looking casually from the road, it may not be obvious that Swifts Hill is an environment rich in wildlife. To the untrained eye, the most obvious things about it are an absence of trees and the yellowish colour of its grass, standing out from the rich greens all around. In fact, Swifts Hill – otherwise known as the Elliott Nature Reserve after the family who transferred it to the Gloucestershire Wildlife Trust in 1967 – is something of a jewel. It is considered one of the county's most beautiful wildflower grasslands, being home to many rare plants and butterflies, some of which are mentioned elsewhere (see 'Flora and Fauna', p.29), as well as some notable fossils. Until the 1930s, this kind of limestone grassland, which gets its colour from never having been ploughed, covered 40 per cent of the Cotswolds; the figure is now down to 2 per cent.

In the past, some say, Swifts Hill was used as a preaching-ground by evangelists – but if so, we have no idea how large were the congregations that climbed up to hear them. In the early 20th century, also, the Hill was sometimes used by gypsies as a gathering-place

The spirit of the Cotswolds... that special panorama of the Slad Valley, taken from the lane as it curves around the base of Swifts Hill

and camp, the old disused quarry offering them some privacy and protection from the prevailing west wind. In *Cider with Rosie*, Laurie Lee commented on the children of his generation at Slad School having an inborn hatred for outcasts. These included "the gypsy boy Rosso, who lived up the quarry where his tribe had encamped for the summer. He had a chocolate-smooth face and crisp black curls, and at first we cold-shouldered him. He was a real outsider (they ate snails, it was said) and his slant Indian eyes repelled us. Then one day, out of hunger, he stole some sandwiches and was given the cane [by the teacher]. Whatever the rights and wrongs of the case, that made him one of us."

According to one Elcombe resident of that time, "Swifts Hill should have been called 'Snakes Hill' — there were so many of them". Today, apart from the naturalists and those climbing up for the breathtaking views from the top, people come mostly to exercise their dogs or to escape from other people: couples parking their cars for clandestine trysts in the quarry, or the so-called joy-riders using it to burn out vehicles they have stolen.

BURIED TREASURE

Somewhere in Elcombe lies hidden treasure, waiting to be discovered by a lucky person (if it hasn't been already). The booty is a bag of precious stones, said to be part of the fortune brought back by 'Old Will' King from gold-prospecting in Australia in the 1920s. The story goes that when he got back to Elcombe, Old Will hid a bag of opals (semi-precious, strictly speaking, but let's not be too pernickety) in the wall along the bridle track leading to the Pitch. And he must have told Louisa Harrison of Habricia Cottage, who called him 'Uncle Bill', for she in turn told the Myles boys, John and David. It set them hunting, but they never found the treasure.

Gwen Wenman, a later resident of Habricia Cottage, says that before she had heard of this story, she was walking along the track one day when she saw a piece of material poking out between the stones of the wall. On examination, she found it was a bag, and in the bag was a collection of dark stones. Thinking it must have been put there for a reason, or possibly by children playing a game, she tied the bag again and replaced it in the wall.

Some time later, Gwen heard about Old Will's opals and realised what she had discovered. So she went back to the wall and started a thorough search, looking into every nook and cranny. But she never rediscovered the Elcombe treasure... or so she says!

Coming from Bisley

The other approach to Elcombe, from the Bisley side, is arguably the more scenic and, for anyone arriving for the first time on a sunny day, even spectacular. It begins with a turning off the main road at the hamlet of Stancombe, not far from Lypiatt Park. Near this turning is the site of the Wittentree Clump, a historic spot where in ancient times the elders of the Bisley Hundred used to hold their assemblies. The word Wittentree is probably Old English, but the experts can't decide whether it derives from *witena-treow,* meaning 'tree of the councillors' or merely from *hwiting-treow,* a wild guelder-rose or water elder tree. The lane is signposted only to Catswood and to Ansteads Farm, now the hub of a thriving business making garden statuary.

As far as Ansteads the lane is high, straight and flat, affording distant views to Bulls Cross and beyond to Painswick. Then it starts to descend between high hedges until curving around in front of the tall, gothic stone gateposts of Catswood Farm, which dates back at least to 1450. A bit further on is the cottage where for many years two ladies bred corgi dogs, from where the lane plunges downhill again and into the woods. Losing the sky, the dark beechwood can seem a mite forbidding after the sunlit uplands. On the left is a track into Papworth's wood, now barred with a felled tree trunk, and the place where Jeannette Tawney had a shed for her pony and trap. A sharp downward bend to the right, followed immediately by a hairpin to the left, where the stony track called King Charles' Lane – once the Bisley-Gloucester main road – goes off straight down the hill into more woods, heading for Steanbridge. Then, descending a short distance from the hairpin, the woods pull back from the road like a stage curtain and the valley is suddenly revealed: a superb vista spread out below, stretching to Stroud and far beyond along the escarpment to the distant River Severn.

Reaching the hamlet
Here Elcombe begins, with Rose Cottage occupying the highest position in the hamlet and looking directly across the valley westwards to Slad. A hundred yards further on, Hillside has a similar outlook, and a bit further, still descending, are the drive to Under Catswood and the bridle track to Yew Tree Cottage, leading further on to the steep path called The Pitch through the centre of the hamlet. A few yards further down the lane, on the right, is the track descending to Furners Farm and Fletchers Knapp, and 150 yards more, passing Springfield Cottage's vegetable garden on the valley side, brings one to the main cluster of cottages. On the left of the Pitch, which comes down between them, are Habricia and Linden Cottages, with Elcombe Cottage below them, and on the right Kenwood Cottage half way up, with Springfield Cottage and Woodside fronting the lane below.

Catswood and Steanbridge

Catswood Farm was part of the Lypiatt Park estate well into the 19th century. According to the book of Gloucestershire place-names, Catswood was first recorded in the 15th century and meant 'a wood haunted by wildcats'. In 1820, the farm's tenant, Joseph Faulks, also held the woodlands of Dunkite Hill Plantation and Tranters Hill. A bit earlier (1777), Catswood and Furners Farm were in the hands of the same William Poulson, but the house at Furners was taxed separately, indicating that Poulson owned it himself or was the tenant of another estate (possibly Steanbridge).

At the bottom of King Charles' Hill, Steanbridge House, Slad, was formerly the site of one of the highest mills in the valley and more recently the seat of the local Squire, who owned much of the land around and who used to invite everyone from Elcombe and The Vatch to his tea parties on special national occasions, notably coronations and armistices. These ceased after the Steanbridge estate was broken up at the beginning of World War II, the house and land being sold separately. During the war, the granddaughters of Ethiopia's Emperor Haile Selassie are said to have stayed at Steanbridge.

So much, then, for our brief tour of Elcombe and its hinterland. There are also, of course, many beautiful walks through the valley and the surrounding countryside, but this is not a guidebook in the conventional sense, so it will be left to readers to explore them. Instead, it is now time to meet some of the people who have been part of, and have enriched, the history of this place.

On the island beside the entrance to Furners Farm the grass is stiff with frost, while the lane curves down towards the spring with Tranters Hill behind

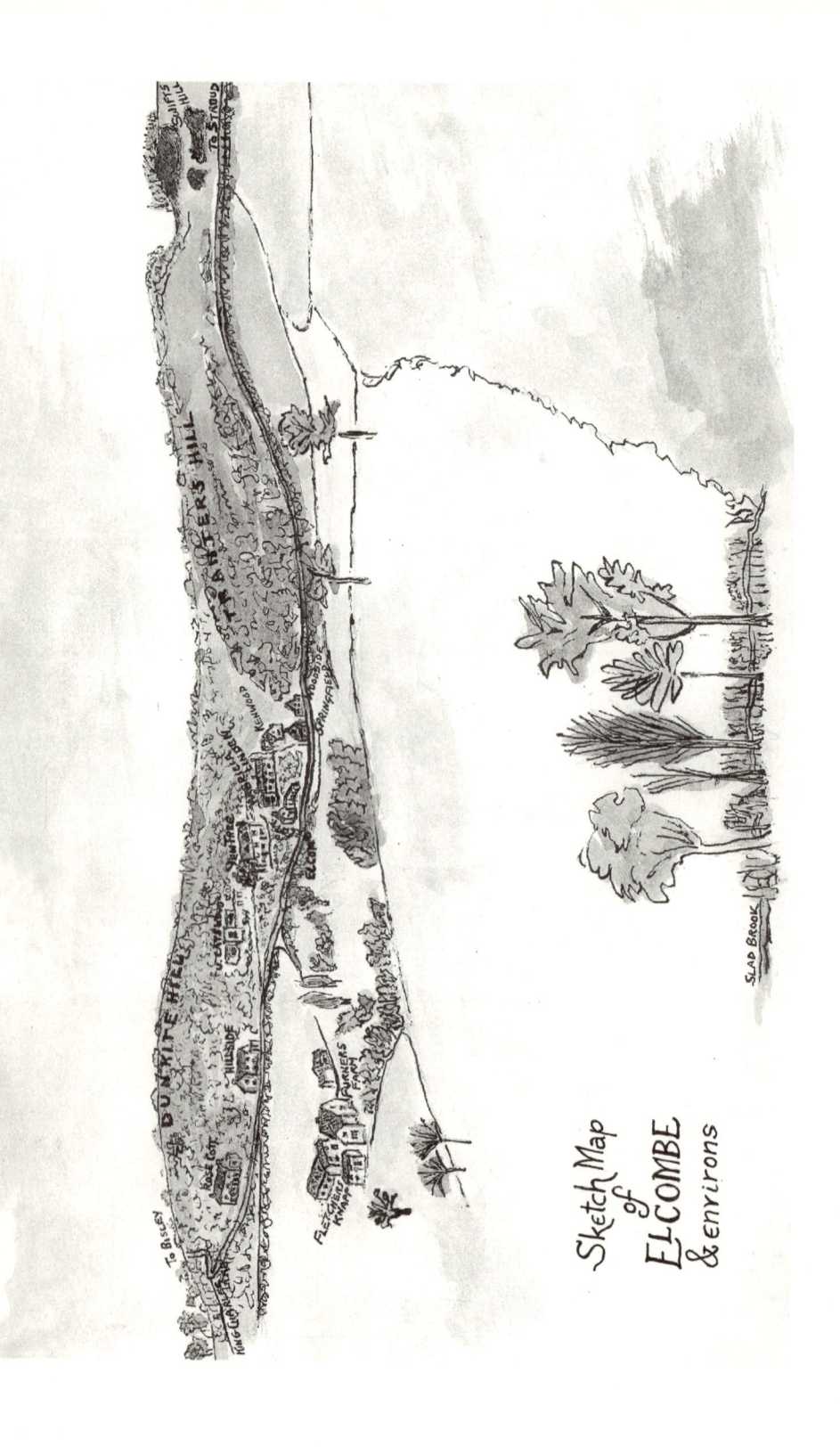

Sketch Map of ELCOMBE & environs

5   Five generations, 25 children
- *The Bartlett Family*

Ferrets. Janet Bartlett's father and grandfather – and many others besides – kept ferrets and used them for hunting rabbits. The ferret, a member of the weasel family, has been used for killing rats and rabbiting since Roman times. "We put nets over the holes when the ferret went in," Janet recounted. "When a rabbit came up I'd grab it and hold it till someone came and pulled its neck. We often lost ferrets. They'd get blocked by the body of a rabbit they'd already killed. My grandfather's favourite ferret was called Lisa."

There have been Bartletts in Bisley since the 16th century (and a Iohannes Bartelet back in 1378), but the first recorded at Elcombe is John, who was born in Cirencester in 1804 and died here in 1875. Starting as an agricultural labourer, he became a carter by 1861 and farmer of 51 acres at Furners in 1871. He married Rachel May in 1836, by whom he had 11 children at two-year intervals: eight daughters, three sons. Two of the three sons died in infancy; the survivor, Thomas (b.1843) married and had six children: three boys, three girls. He was a cloth worker in Stroud in 1865 but moved to Elcombe in 1868. One must assume that he didn't fancy taking over Furners, or else his father didn't think he was the right one for it. The fact is, two of John Bartlett's daughters married two brothers, Thomas and George Partridge, and it was they who in due course took over Furners Farm after John B's death.

Thomas's youngest son, Arthur Sam, was born in 1873, probably in Elcombe, according to Janet. He married Mary Mutton and had seven children – five boys, two girls. The three eldest boys, Ernest, Edward and Reginald, fought in World War I. Sam and his other two sons, Ted and Harry, worked at Townsends Flour Mill in Stroud, making cattle cake, while his daughters, Alice and Ethel, went into domestic service at one of the grander houses in The Vatch.

[45]

Sam also kept pigs and chickens in his garden and farmer Fletcher allowed him to make a hole in the garden wall so the hens could run across the road into his field. There's a fine photograph of Sam on The Pitch with one of his sows and a litter of piglets (see p.27). Of his children, several moved away from Elcombe, but Reginald and Francis (Frank, b.1906) stayed. When he was young, Frank often played truant from school, but there was one job he had to do: when he got home in the afternoon, his regular task was to take Sam's pigs for a walk in the woods.

Nearly every Saturday night, after they'd had a few drinks, Sam Bartlett and Fred Green's father, Charlie, would end by having a punch-up. The Tucks also didn't get on with the Bartletts. One night, Reg Bartlett (Sam's third son) was attacked on Swifts Hill and seriously injured. He was taken to hospital by Stan Fletcher and stayed there several weeks but never really recovered. He died in 1943 at age 43.

When Sam Bartlett had the cottage, the triangle of land beyond Yew Tree Cottage was also part of its land. That triangle had previously belonged in 1869 to a Samuel Webb (the Webb family had been in the area since at least 1561 – not to mention being the present owners of Knapp House farm), and before him to a William Fletcher. But it is not known if these two were also owners of Springfield Cottage.

Arthur Sam and Mary Bartlett

A lifetime with cows

After the Partridges left Furners, Frank went to work for the farm's new owners, the Fletchers (whose son, Stan, took over in time from his father). He spent his life as a cowman on what had been his grandfather's farm, living in the cottage which has become Fletcher's Knapp. Frank married Elsie Critchley and their daughter, Janet, was born in 1937.

Janet Bartlett spent her first 33 years at Elcombe until her father retired and moved to Ruscombe in 1970. Recalling her childhood, Janet says: "A lot of the time we used to go woodin' along Catswood, gathering sticks. I played games with the Bodenhams [of Yew Tree Cottage]. We had to invent our own games, there was not much in the way of toys or material things."

Was it a happy childhood? "Well, I suppose – but not so happy as some of them has it now, because there was rationing – and we had to walk to Slad School. I stayed there till I was eight, then Uplands, for which there was a bus from The Vatch. When I was 14, Rodborough Secondary Modern opened. We had a bus to Stroud but then had to walk from Stroud to Rodborough."

Like others, Janet had special memories of the celebrations in the valley at the end of World War II. "I remember VE [Victory in Europe] Day – we went to the Woolpack and there were a lot of people and they were all going to the Ritz for music and dancing." In 1953, she went to a Coronation Party at Steanbridge, where, in the traditions of the Squire, there was a festive tea for all the people of Slad, The Vatch and Elcombe.

After leaving school, her first job was at Stonehouse, on the other side of Stroud. Speaking in 1995, she said: "I've done a lot of different work – a lot in the printing trade, Stroud brewery…and now I'm cleaning. I've met a lot of interesting people."

Janet Bartlett at Furners, 1958

When he died in 1976, Fletcher's will included a bequest of £150 to Frank for his 'long and faithful service', but since Frank had predeceased him Fletcher's sisters refused to pay it to his widow. "I'll never forgive the Fletchers for that," said Janet 20 years later.

The Bartletts were inevitably linked by marriage to other families in the valley. Janet had an uncle, Richard Durn, who was a close relative of the Richard Durn at Minden Cottage in 1900, and through whom she was distantly related both to Elizabeth White, licensee of the old Star Inn, and to Elsie Durn, postmistress at Uplands.

A VERY SPECIAL GOAT - AND OTHER PETS

Rabbits were a staple ingredient of the cooking pot in old Elcombe, and there was no shortage of them in the surrounding fields. Not everyone had a gun, so a favoured method of catching them was with ferrets. By the 1950s, however, rabbiting was dying out.

With the demise of working animals, family pets began to take over. Several of these were propelled to stardom in Graham Wenman's "Elcombe Epics", including Whiz the goat, Henry the chocolate labrador, Nyger the very black cat and numerous others. One of the stories about Whiz began as follows:

"Whiz is a very special goat. He was brought up in Slad Vicarage and fed with a babies bottle when his mother died. He watched Television with the Vicar's children at an early age and is, therefore, very observant, and his present owner Goatman takes him for a ride on the front seat of his station-wagon up to his son's farm at Minchinhampton where Whiz often stays for the summer. In the winter he lives in the old shed in Goatman's orchard.

"Goatman plays the drums in a dance band and, when he practises 'Big Noise Blew in from Winnetga' on holidays, Whiz gets quite excited and rushes around on his chain. On Sunday afternoons he gets taken for a walk by the family."

Whiz and friends (in this case, Leonora and Cicci)

Another favourite in Elcombe around that time was George, an extremely obese black labrador from Catswood Farm, who more than anything loved cattle cake and calf's milk. When everyone was busy at the farm he would come to Elcombe to visit; easy enough to come down the steep lane, but, as he got fatter and fatter, not so easy to get home again. One friendly couple, the Roffes, sometimes provided him with a taxi service, putting him in their car and driving him back up the hill.

6 THE LAST OF THE OLD TIMERS
Bill Tuck

He was a real old country character, of a kind we shall never see again, and when he died in 1970 it was the symbolic demise of all those like him who for centuries had embodied the best of England's rural way of life. Born in 1877 and raised in the nearby village of Amberley, Bill Tuck fought in the Boer War (1899-1902), became a stonemason, then fought again in World War I before resuming his trade.

As a mason, Bill Tuck was immensely proud of the houses and walls he had built in the valley and round about. Proud, too, of his son, Caleb, who set up in business as a haulier and did well for himself. But he was less lucky in love. His first wife, after giving him a son, drowned herself in a pond at the bottom of King Charles' Hill, as popularly recorded in Laurie Lee's *Cider with Rosie*; and his second, Elsie, was a strange woman who became a Jehovah's Witness and eventually, in John Papworth's phrase, "outlived several of her faculties".

Bill survived them both and is remembered in his latter years as "a blue-eyed, apple-cheeked old man, whose voice and speech were peculiar and delightful fruits of Gloucestershire rural history." He spoke in the old second person singular - for example, "Thi' bist" = Thou be-est = You are. And he was the last living person in the hamlet who might have complained about "wunt hillocks" – being the old local name for molehills – or who might have complimented you on your "peasipouse", which were peas and beans grown together as a crop.

Well into his 80s, Bill Tuck was still working from home, carving stone ornaments – sundials, birdbaths and the like. And not far short of 90, he would still take his ancient bicycle for a daily ride to the pub in Slad, where he was reputed to consume anything upto 12 pints of

[49]

beer at a session. He would push the bike up the steep hill on the way back, then mount it at the top of Swifts Hill for the final free-wheel descent to Elcombe along Trantershill Wood. Unfortunately, the story goes, the alcohol sometimes affected his navigation, so that more than once he landed in the hedge or the ditch. On one side, at least, it was his own ditch, for at some point he or Caleb had bought Tranter's Hill. After them, the wood was bought by Laurie Lee, who could see it on the skyline from the cottage down below in the valley where he spent his early years.

The shop and the spring

The Tucks' was a little one-up, one-down cottage with a gable and a stained-glass window. On one side was an extension where for some years Elsie ran a small general shop, selling milk, cigarettes, potatoes and a few things from the Co-op; on the other, a tiny workshop where he prepared stone and an ivy-covered privy. The privy, as Papworth records, had "a caved-in roof (which must have made squatting there a draughty business) and in front was a beautifully kept grass bank veering down to the spring by the roadside." This was where, until the mid-1950s, everyone came to fetch their drinking water – effectively the village green and the social hub of the hamlet.

According to Graham Wenman, Tuck apparently used to hit Elsie sometimes, because she often had big bruises. We know very little about levels of domestic violence in rural communities of his or earlier generations, but it can safely be assumed that women often bore the physical brunt of their husbands' misery or frustrations. Elsie may have been no exception.

Bill Tuck also had an idiosyncratic way of talking about the past. When reminiscing about "the war" and the damage caused to Painswick's church spire, it would be found that he was talking of the Civil War of more than 300 years ago. In his later years, Tuck would declare that the best time of his life was as a soldier in the trenches in 1916, when there was a brief truce for Christmas and the Germans came across the front line to join them for drinks. Wenman found this sad: "What does it say of the quality of the rest of his life?" We shall never know, but perhaps for Bill Tuck those Christmas drinks had a more profound meaning to do with the virtues of reconciliation and recognising the common humanity even of one's enemies.

Like most of his generation, Tuck was a keen vegetable gardener and, as well as the small garden behind Woodside Cottage, he had the benefit

Bill Tuck in uniform, World War I

of the only plot on the south side of the lane. After his death, this plot was bought by Miss Ibferson next door and has since belonged to Springfield Cottage. As he grew older, John Papworth recalled, Tuck became increasingly confused about his age and also his birthday:

> "At first this was probably deliberate when he discovered how easily people would give him half a crown, or if in the pub, a drink, on hearing that that particular day was his annual milestone. But later on I think he was genuinely muddled and towards the end he never failed to remind me of his nativity every time we met. By then I had ceased to fall for it, although the trickle of unsuspecting visitors to the hamlet who stopped to chat with him by his well-tended spring rarely failed to part from him feeling they had purchased virtue and goodwill, and a much nicer opinion of themselves, very cheaply in token of a few coins to mark what they supposed was the great occasion."

Death among the lilies

In the first edition of *Cider with Rosie*, telling the story of the drowning of Tuck's first wife, Florence, in Steanbridge Pond in 1922, Laurie Lee called her 'Miss Fluck'. But there were objections that this made her too identifiable, so in subsequent editions she became 'Miss Flynn'. Though he was only eight years old at the time of the tragedy, Laurie's later account described her poignantly as "a solitary, off-beat beauty, whose mute, distressed, life-abandoned image remains with me till this day." He added that she was tall, consumptive and pale as thistledown, a flock-haired pre-Raphaelite stunner, and she had a small wind-harp which played tunes to itself by swinging in the boughs of her apple trees. She gave the boys apples and stroked their hair with long, yellow fingers. Her long, stone-white and tapering face, he said, seemed as cool as a churchyard angel. A few days before her death, she confided to Laurie's mother that she was being bothered by the sick spirit of her dead mother: "She don't let me alone at nights".

Florence was found one morning, floating among the lilies in Steanbridge pond, by the young milkman Fred Green, her next-door neighbour and Tuck's nephew. By Laurie Lee's account, she was naked and her eyes wide open. Fred ran back to the farm and told them, and they came and pulled her out with a hay rake. She was carried home on a hurdle. Laurie Lee implies that 'Miss Flynn' was a little free with her favours. If not that, one infers from the book that there must have been something that prompted his mother to remark to Laurie, after they met her in the lane, that "there are others more wicked, poor soul."

However, Laurie Lee's version of the tragedy – and the illustration which depicts poor Florence floating on her back with long hair spread out, just like every picture of Ophelia – begins to look a trifle romanticised when one reads the report of the coroner's inquest, held at Tuck's cottage the following day.

At the time of her death, Florence was 42 – a little mature, one might think, to be a 'pre-Raphaelite stunner' in the memory of an eight-year-old when he grew up. When she had married Bill twenty years earlier, she was one of the many in country areas who still could not write their own name, signing the register instead with the customary X.

The inquest was told that Florence had been in ill-health for some time, and although she had never threatened to take her own life she sometimes suffered intense head-pains as the result of a fall years earlier. The previous night, Tuck said, he had woken up at about 3 a.m. to find his wife getting dressed. She said she was going 'round the back' and would only be 10 minutes; however, a few minutes later their son, Caleb, came to tell him she had left the house. They both went searching for her until the time she was found.

Farmer Cecil Close of Steanbridge, who retrieved the body from the pond after being alerted by Fred Green, told the coroner that Florence had been floating in a crouching position, with the back of her head and shoulders above the water. Not quite like Ophelia.

The walk from Elcombe to Steanbridge is about a mile across the fields, and when she got there, according to police evidence, she would have had to climb a four-foot high wire fence. The inquest jury returned a verdict of death from drowning whilst temporarily insane.

Elsie's odd ways

Tuck's second wife, Elsie, was already living in Elcombe, a few steps up The Pitch, before their marriage. Once installed with Bill at Woodside, she seldom ventured beyond her garden gate, relying on the weekly Stroud Co-operative van for her provisions rather than taking the bus into town. But with a fingernail as long as a witch's she would beckon to any neighbour filling their buckets at the spring and regale them with warnings of impending doom.

Standards of home-making and hygiene were different then – and Elsie's were almost non-existent. Despite having six cats, the cottage was overrun with mice. She never cut her hair or nails, so some of her fingernails were inches long and her hair was a source of wonder: a matted, bouffant mass piled on top of her head. Papworth described her as having "a large, firm mouth containing a prominent, solitary, dark brown, lower front molar." Evidently fascinated by it, he made that tooth the centrepiece of his little pen portrait:

> "Her speech would tumble and slither around that monument to her former dental glory like an alpine stream coursing some huge obstructive boulder, and nearly all of it would be concerned with religion of a particularly primitive and fundamentalist kind. She was in fact a Jehovah's Witness, having been converted by one of the area visitors who call at every house in the entire valley two or three times a year.
>
> "At great length and in graphic detail, while my buckets filled and overflowed, she would explain why and how the end of the

world was at hand, although she had no inkling at all as to how our scientists, technicians, planners and experts of all kinds are working like beavers to make her ignorant predictions a reality. The last time I spoke with her I left her at her gate declaiming with hoarse and and warmingly insistent fanaticism, 'All the people are gathering, Mr Papworth, all the people are gathering'. I learned later a Witness rally was being held, a prosaic enough explanation perhaps, but her words were the very stuff of ballad, myth and legend."

In her younger days, Les Brown of Hillside remembered Elsie as "a fine country girl" who worked at a mill in Stroud and walked there and back every day. But in the end she couldn't or wouldn't even take care of the basics. A nurse came to wash her, because she wouldn't do it herself, but she refused to have her hair washed. The nurse appealed for help to Evie Wenman (Habricia Cottage), and in the end they decided to cut it. That's when they found that Elsie's hair was full of mouse-droppings. Eventually she was taken away to a mental institution, and not long afterwards Bill had to go into an old people's home, where he died. In a real sense his demise marked the end of a way of life in harmony with the natural world - a harmony which, however meagre in material wealth, was the unifying force in the building of Elcombe and so many communities like it.

7 'THE GREATEST MAN IN ENGLAND'
R H Tawney

The most illustrious resident in Elcombe's history so far – a man passionate for social reform, whose ideas resonated across much of Britain's 20th century – was R H Tawney.

Tawney was the outstanding radical thinker and teacher of his generation. Social philosopher, historian and pioneer of adult education, he influenced governments and was a key contributor to the concepts and architecture of the Welfare State. On his 80th birthday in 1960, an editorial in *The Times* declared: "No man alive has put more people in his spiritual and intellectual debt than has Richard Henry Tawney."

Elcombe was essentially a holiday home for Tawney, given his many work commitments in London and further afield. His purchase of Rose Cottage in 1928, which incidentally must have made him the hamlet's first 'weekender', coincided with his election as President of the Workers' Educational Association. And three years later he was appointed Professor at the London School of Economics. But his wife Jeannette, a larger-than-life character, spent a lot of time at Elcombe and is the subject of the chapter that follows.

Harry Tawney and Jeannette Beveridge had both been born in India, and in the same year, 1880. Tawney's father, a Sanscrit scholar, was the Principal of a college in Calcutta. In due course he sent his son to Rugby School and then to Balliol College, Oxford, where he met Jeannette's brother, William, the future Lord Beveridge. When Tawney completed his Oxford studies with a 2nd class degree, his father inquired tersely: "How do you propose to wipe out this disgrace?" The rest of his life was the answer, and when he died in 1962 the Labour leader Hugh Gaitskell declared: "Looking back quite objectively, I think he was the best man I have ever known."

From university, Tawney went to Toynbee Hall in London, where he undertook a mixture of social work and social research, writing many pamphlets against the blight of child labour. He joined the executive of the recently-founded Workers' Educational Association (WEA) in 1905 and the Fabian Society in 1906. Just before the outbreak of World War I he married Jeannette and they moved to Mecklenburgh Square, near London University, where according to his biographer Ross Terrill, Jeannette "hovered over a ménage of total chaos, which no one set adrift in it even for a day could easily forget".

When war broke out in 1914, Tawney's university background would normally have gained him a commission, but he chose to enlist as a private. Shot in the stomach in Flanders, he barely survived, but while he was recovering in a field hospital the Archbishop of Canterbury paid him a visit. Said the archbishop to the matron: "Look after him. He is the greatest man in England". Said the matron to the patient: "Mr Tawney, why didn't you tell me you was a gentleman?"

Pioneer of adult education
After the war he campaigned for educational reforms. Appointed to a royal commission on the coal mines in 1919, he became a national figure arguing the miners' case for nationalisation. His ideas were shelved until after the next war, when they were implemented by the government of Clement Attlee. He held the presidency of the WEA for 17 years, during which time he contributed largely to giving working men a sense of their dignity as citizens. In the same period he was a frequent contributor to The (Manchester) Guardian with articles on education.

As professor at the London School of Economics, one of his colleagues was the medieval scholar Eileen Power, "for whom", Terrill coyly notes, "his affection would be hard to over-estimate". She and Tawney had co-edited several books in the 1920s and her death in 1940 was a deep shock to him. Terrill says: "She had been his intimate friend, as Jeannette well knew, and at times an inspiration." Shortly before she died, in a letter to her brother, Jeannette mentions a visit to Eileen Power's house in Cambridge, which was "quite delightful. It is modern but also most comfortable."

The Tawneys and Bob outside Rose Cottage in the 1930s

Tawney had some previous connections with the Cotswolds before coming to Rose Cottage. On leave from the trenches in World War I, he would come with a friend on fishing trips to this area. And in 1934, wearing his economic historian's hat, he wrote a study of employment in Gloucestershire in 1608, showing that rural and agricultural society were by no means synonymous.

The Second World War did not begin too well for the Tawneys. In the autumn of 1940, their house in Mecklenburgh Square was first damaged by time bombs and then almost demolished by what Jeannette described as "a vast enemy missile at the back of the house". There were several other direct hits nearby and "several houses demolished on the Grays Inn Road side of the square." A bit later they took refuge for a night at a house in nearby Gower Street and "I was just saying to Henry how quiet it all was when our shutters were blown open and the whole house shook. It was evidently a bomb in Tottenham Court Road."

The bombing meant they had to try to rescue their possessions and "Henry's books are a great problem as no one will handle them and the packing case problem is so acute." Writing from Elcombe, Jeannette says, "I have been dashing up to London by car and retrieving what I can. The problem of what to do with the books when salvaged is still unsolved. This little cottage will hardly accommodate any of them."

But a month later, the transportation problem at least had been solved. To substitute for unavailable packing cases, they had found, of all things, pheasant baskets, normally used for transporting live birds. Jeannette records that the baskets were "sized 3ft by 2ft by one, which the pheasant farm proprietor was not using owing to the lack of demand for stock birds". (The English gentry now had bigger game in their sights.) Fifty of these baskets were airfreighted to London and loaded up for the journey to Gloucestershire. The following year, the Tawneys were given some relief when he was appointed Labour Adviser to the British Embassy in Washington (1941-42). When they came back, they brought with them — probably thanks to Jeannette's acquisitive streak — a large supply of American tinned food, including many 14-lb. tins of coffee beans. These were stored in a shed lower down the garden, but it was not weatherproof and many unused tins simply rusted over the years. More than a decade later, the next owner of the cottage inherited this hoard of mildewed coffee beans, but at least it kept him warm for his first winter, being used as fuel for the fire.

Tawney eventually retired from LSE in 1949. In all, he wrote 11 books. If *Religion and the Rise of Capitalism* is perhaps the best known, there is still much gold to be mined from others such as *Equality*, *The Acquisitive Society* and *The Radical Tradition*.

The comfort of old clothes

Tawney never had much money, partly perhaps because he really didn't want it and because he gave much of what he had to WEA projects and other causes. Another reason was that Jeannette had a habit of squandering money on extravagances. In any case, he dressed scruffily and didn't mind admitting it. He once remarked: "I am told by a candid friend that, before smoking in public so superior a cigar, I must buy new clothes or I shall be suspected of having stolen it." Or as Jeannette put it in 1948: "The burglars have again invaded our London flat. Mercifully, the quality of Henry's clothes prevent their being stolen, so that was a comfort".

One reason for agreeing to three months of lectures at the University of Chicago in 1939 was that it was well paid ($5000) and he needed the money to pay off debts that he and Jeannette had incurred. Two years later, when he went to the Washington embassy, the Tawneys luggage, following by sea, was torpedoed, so they hunted for second-hand clothes, wishing to spend as much of possible of their dollar income on food parcels for English friends. When in his 70s, Terrill reports, the landlord of his London flat was sometimes hovering over him for the rent, which he could not always pay. When he died he left an estate of just £7,000.

More peasant than peer

In 1933, the Prime Minister of the day, Ramsey MacDonald, offered Tawney a peerage. His reply, according to Ross Terrill, was cryptic: "Thank you for your letter. What harm have I ever done to the Labour Party? Yours sincerely." Another version has it that he added: "Even a mad dog does not tie a tin can to its own tail."

Rather than as a lord in ermine, Tawney saw himself as "a peasant displaced from the soil". He became a well-known figure in our valley, often out walking with a Cotswold peg and stout boots, exchanging stories with locals at one of the pubs (Terrill says 'the Stroud pub' but presumably the Star or Woolpack) or sometimes passing jauntily by with a wave from the pony and trap.

"The cottage was a charming slum," writes Terrill, though apparently not from first-hand knowledge. "There being no automatic toilet, a patch of ground near the dwelling could give off terrible odours." In her usual fashion, he adds, Jeannette blended luxury and squalor. On one occasion she vastly over-ordered strawberries and cream for a tea party, but she was a good cook and taught Patrick Gordon Walker, a Labour Party front-bencher, to make a good omelette.

When his books finally came from London after the bombing in those 50 pheasant baskets, Tawney made a new home for his library in two henhouses – one of them still there – at the top of the steep garden behind the cottage. Also during the war, hearing of some working-class friends with nowhere to live (presumably also bombed out), he sent them a telegram inviting them to Elcombe. They came with an unexpected bevy of children and also ended up living in the henhouse.

After being bombed out of Mecklenburgh Square, the Tawneys found a new abode nearby, which Terrill describes as "two chickenhouses with the outward appearance of a public toilet" approached by steps behind the Russell Hotel. Visitors described it as squalid, but Tawney didn't mind that. "I didn't know hens lived so luxuriously," he is reported to have said when he moved in.

Eventually, due to Jeannette's continuing ill-health, the Tawneys sold Rose Cottage in 1955. Its new owner was another campaigner for social and political reform, though of a somewhat different ilk. This was John Papworth, who later took holy orders (having being thrown out of the Communist Party) and who, over the next 20 years, made his own distinctive contribution to the annals of Elcombe.

8 WHEN HARRY MET TUTU
The redoubtable Mrs Tawney

Surprisingly, perhaps, they weren't introduced by her brother, William, who had been a close friend of Tawney at Oxford. Instead, Harry met Jeannette Beveridge a few years later when he was working for the Children's Country Holiday Fund. They married in 1909 and it was almost another 20 years before they acquired Rose Cottage.

Jeannette - known to her intimates as Tutu - was one of nature's eccentrics: impulsive and often extravagant with it. Always loyal to Tawney and supportive of his principles, she was an intelligent woman in her own right and became one of the first women factory inspectors in England. But, dogged by ill health, she was somewhat mortified at the outbreak of World War II when the Home Office declined to give her her old job back, saying it would now be too strenuous. It meant that she had to register for the war effort as an 'unpaid domestic help'.

Through most of her time at Rose Cottage, Jeannette wrote frequent letters to her brother, who would later become a household name as Lord Beveridge. Her side of the correspondence is preserved with Tawney's papers at the London School of Economics, and it contains some fascinating detail of their life in the valley as well as frequent appeals for financial help to compensate for the modest lifestyle of an impecunious professor's wife.

In May 1933, Jeannette wrote: "Dearest Will, I am writing to say again thank you so much for bringing us down in such luxury and comfort [in your car]. We are so grateful. It was a lovely sunny day to remember and the beauty of the country was a real refreshment to me... Mr Freeman has been along to see me today and was anxious to know how I liked the place. He says it meant a great deal of planning but that the designs were mine and he thought I'd been very clever in working out the verandah so well and closing the old passage... Your

[61]

and my scheme for a window has developed into a wonderfully nice thing. The window alone would never have met the situation, though it would have been a great advantage. Of course, old cottages and stone ones are a problem – but it's excellent now."

The next day she wrote again: "Thank you ever so much for your generous contribution to the cottage reconditioning," without which she would never have undertaken the scheme which had exceeded her wildest dreams. "It's lovely to be sitting as I now am in the sunny window with the French doors open and the sun streaming in on me. We are still in rather a muddle but every day things are discovered and we really have been lucky in our workmen and our Mrs Harrison." She also thanks him for carpets – an essential as her room now has a concrete floor replacing one with severe dry rot.

She had been having one of her recurrent bouts of illness and had a live-in nurse at the time, but the following month she reports, "I am really much better now… I have been making cakes and gooseberry jelly and endless sewing jobs – curtains, etc. The cottage is so nice." She invites Will to come and stay – the cottage now has "a really good visitor's bedroom and dressing room", though she herself prefers to sleep outside (in the garden or in a shed?) on a bed he has given her.

Both the Tawneys were from upper middle-class backgrounds, but while Harry at Elcombe enjoyed mixing with the ordinary village folk – the kind of people he was involved with in the WEA – Jeannette made friends more readily with a somewhat higher society. In the same letter, she relates with pleasure: "I'm being treated by Harry to a car for Lady Ware's Garden Party." It seems the Tawneys and the Wares became friends, for in 1938 Sir Fabian Ware (possibly a diplomat?) paid a visit to Rose Cottage shortly after returning from an interview with Italy's head of state, Mussolini.

Saving a life
In November 1933, Jeannette wrote that "we have shut up the cottage for the winter. We shall probably not go there now till spring." Their puppy, Bob, had been sent to a farmer to be trained. By the next April she was back, driven down by William, and on the very day of her return she became the central character in a drama of life and death.

"After you left," she wrote a few days later, "I found that poor Mr Harrison had not been found anywhere. I had a brilliant idea, viz. that Mrs Michael Sadleir [of Througham Court] should be telephoned and asked if she would bring out her bloodhounds, which she breeds and one of which had been the prize-winner at Crufts. She agreed eagerly and willingly but said nothing could be done till the morning as no one could go at night into the woods with dogs. So on the morning of Friday they set out at 8am and one dog at once seemed to have found a trail which Mrs Sadleir followed. In front of her she suddenly saw a man's leg projecting from the Slad brook. There Mr Harrison was found at 8:45am. He was alive and quite conscious and clear as to who helped him out – viz. his son and he was taken straight to hospital where he remained for three nights and was all right. He then went to the Infirmary where chronic cases are taken. He'd been missing about 40 hours so it's very wonderful. I'm so thankful that you brought me that Thursday because if I'd not come nothing would have been done and the poor man would have died from exposure and cold. He had slipped and could not get up. I tell you as it's really an interesting story. I feel everyone should hear of the possibility of using dogs – not only for criminals and corpses, for which at present the police alone reserve them. They have no right to use dogs nor to search under 48 hours of disappearance. It has cheered me immensely to feel I really was instrumental in saving his life."

In case Mr Harrison needed cheering up during his convalescence at the Workhouse Infirmary, Jeannette thoughtfully provided him with copies of the humorous magazine *Punch*, to which William had given her a subscription. Without more research, one can only surmise that Mr Harrison was related to "our Mrs Harrison" (the possessive pronoun suggesting a domestic help) who figures elsewhere in Jeannette's correspondence. Mrs H must have been with them in some capacity for 11 years until 1944, when Jeannette records that "our beloved Mrs Harrison has had a stroke and will never work again". This suggests that the Mrs H in question may have been Louisa Harrison, who lived at Habricia Cottage until her death in 1947.

The Mrs Sadleir of Througham Court was the wife of the writer Michael Sadleir, who in 1922 had found the grand house empty and derelict since the sale of Lypiatt estates. A few years later Sadleir – best known for his book 'Fanny by Gaslight' – bought the house and engaged the architect Norman Jewson to restore it.

The pony and trap

A few months later, the next saga of Rose Cottage was the acquisition of a pony and trap. This again was Jeannette's idea – and it became something by which the Tawneys were remembered many years afterwards: the pair of them sailing almost majestically along the highways and byways around Slad, waving cheerily to everyone they passed.

In reply to William, who has offered her a refrigerator, she writes: "Much as I might like one at some other time, at the moment my most urgent and pressing need is some sort of trap and place in which to keep it and a pony, to enable me to have the pony that Harry has been chasing for me all the summer. By an odd coincidence the ideal one is offered to us today. It has been approved by the vet and is a charming pony. We had felt we must not have it this year as our finances are very badly depleted with my illness and the unlet flat and a dropped ceiling and losses by that of £200, but feel that if Harry will give me the pony and you will give me the £20 which is I understand the price of the refrigerator we should decide to have the pony. The pony is very good

Only about 20 years after the hillsides were clear-felled, natural woodland growth had taken over again by the 1960s

and gentle. If you are willing to give me the £20 towards the trap and stable Harry will I think feel justified in spending the £20 demanded for the pony, and we are told that that is quite a reasonable price for it. Ponies, by reason of not being bred, have now an enhanced value. The farmer selling the pony is willing to work after it free during the winter, so we should not have to make provision for that." Jeannette concludes that if he is prepared to convert his fridge offer into a trap and stable, "I accept it most appreciatively for birthday and Christmas."

Four days later, she has already received her brother's agreement to this deal and she pens another letter to tell him that "I shall have to arrange about a trap when I can get a chance of going either to Gloucester or Cheltenham. The owner of the pony…will lend me his trap for a few weeks." In fact, it took about three months to find what she wanted, but the effort was worthwhile. "The trap hunt was a most interesting and unique experience… We have had ever so many voluntary searchers on the job." And by the summer of '35, she was going out frequently for pony trap rides and "the whole thing is an immense delight to me". Two years later, Will coughed up another £10.17.0. to have the trap overhauled and new tyres fitted. Jeannette continued with her excursions and later reported to him: "I feel very superior to be possessed of a trap and pony and am often greeted with cheers as I go along."

Before the outbreak of World War II, a government official came to Slad to commandeer horses. Jeannette was afraid that her pony, Kitty, would be taken away, and was therefore relieved when the man told her it would be of 'no use'. The purpose the horses were wanted for is not explained, but Kitty evidently decided to celebrate her avoidance of conscription. Soon afterwards she was found to be in foal, to Jeannette's slight consternation. "It will be a bother," she says, "as we know nothing of her dates or size of stallion." In September that year, however, the problem seems to have been overcome. Perhaps it was solved by the exchange of Kitty for another pony, because only two years later – just before the Tawneys left for their stint in Washington – the one they then owned collapsed and had to be shot. During a stopover in the Azores, Jeannette wrote to her brother with the sad news, adding that the animal had been found to be "nearer 20 than 12 as we had thought". At the age of 18, Kitty would presumably have been well past her foal-by date.

When life settled down after the war, Jeannette was in her mid-60s and her letters make no mention of any wish to restore the pony and trap.

Come rain, come shine

The weather was not a major feature of Jeannette's letters, but today's Elcombe generation will be consoled to know that it was no less variable 70 years ago. In September 1934, she noted: "We have had lots of rain and the garden is grateful." The following August: "Here we have no water and are longing for rain, which comes near and then passes us by." And two weeks later: "We have no signs of rain here and the dust and drought are becoming serious problems for everyone." Water, of course, had to be carried up from the spring, which was beside the lowest cottages in the hamlet, whereas Rose Cottage was and remains the most elevated. So it was quite a climb. Like others, Tawney had a wooden yoke for this purpose, with a bucket suspended on each end, but it was heavy work. "We find the water-carrying a lot of bother," Jeannette said. "We attempt to carry some with the pony, but it is quite incredible the amount of water that splashes out over everything."

For the next two or three years, they spend Christmas at Elcombe and in December 1938 "we are snowed up here and are quite enjoying the scene. The cottage is very warm on the whole… The trees were exquisite yesterday with their frosting."

The 1930s were the Tawneys' best years at Rose Cottage, and they spent quite a lot of time there together. It was also a period of many innovations and new domestic conveniences. In 1936, to the embossed cottage notepaper Jeannette added 'Tel. Painswick 207' – and within a year it had become 'Painswick 2207'. Theirs was probably only the second telephone in Elcombe after the Fletchers at Furners Farm, considering that Fletchers Knapp, which was then part of the farm, still has the number 2206 (now prefixed with 81-).

Around the same time, thanks to brother Will's generosity, Jeannette acquired a motorised sewing machine and a wireless. The first of these (and the proposed refrigerator) could hardly have run on batteries, so what form of power generation did they have? Whatever it was, it evidently did not provide for electric lights or heaters, otherwise Jeannette wouldn't have been so delighted when mains electricity finally arrived in the 1950s. In the meantime, the sewing machine motor was "a great boon as the doctors won't allow me to work a treadle machine any more".

For her birthday in 1936, Jeannette asked her brother for a 500-gallon water tank, for which she had obtained an estimate of £10.12.0. "Is this about the amount you had generously contemplated expending on me?" she inquires. In fact, the final cost came to £17.15.0 (70% over estimate), but one must assume that William graciously met it, since there is no evidence of his refusing her anything. He also bought her a 'knife machine', a handbag, and contributed to a fur coat. When he invited her to choose a birthday present the following year, she told him: "I should love to have an arm chair for the cottage, to sit on near the fire. It must not be too enormous...but it should be longish on the seat and wide enough to accommodate Harry. The upholstery should be green or brown but not blue – and please not rexine or leather as the cat destroys that in a week."

Compared with London, one continuing drawback of the cottage in this period, Jeannette noted, was "the lack of indoor conveniences". This regretfully meant that she could not invite her brother to stay, because he was recuperating from some ailment and "it is not fit for the disabled when the weather gets colder."

The outbreak of war
Just at the outbreak of World War II, repairs were carried out to Elcombe Lane, which must have been in poor condition since Jeannette writes to her brother in December '39: "The lane has been mended so that the next time you come to see me you will have to exhibit much less than your ordinary skill". Not long afterwards, Tranter's Hill – then a pine plantation, not the natural mixed woodland that we see today – was clear cut to provide pit props for the coal mines. Is it possible that the lane was resurfaced to make that job easier?

The wartime blackout – which meant that no houses should show lights after dark to avoid helping enemy planes – presented another problem. The Tawneys were still sleeping out and must have needed the help of a torch to get from the house to their shed at bedtime. Jeannette records: "Our sleeping out is extremely difficult to maintain with the lighting restrictions, and our parson's wife – thinking us still away – reported our flashes in the garden to the Chief Constable, suspecting our cottage of harbouring spies! So once again the old rubbish is dug up." What the 'old rubbish' might be, she does not confide – presumably some local gossip about why they should want to sleep in the garden – but it wasn't dug up by the Stroud News, which had no mention of the Tawneys in its column about people charged with breaking the blackout regulations. As for harbouring spies, that could be said to have been the speciality of their successor at Rose Cottage, John Papworth – a tale we will get to later.

In the interests of national security, personal letters were no longer private and in December 1940 Jeannette told her brother: "There seems to be a rigorous censor at work here in Stroud, and letters from Scotland get opened as well as those from abroad."

After their return from Washington in 1942, the Tawneys acquired a new London flat to replace the bombed-out Mecklenburgh Square. Jeannette described it as "an amusing little place immediately behind the Russell Square Hotel." As mentioned earlier, Tawney's biographer, Ross Terrill, was less complimentary, likening it to two chicken coops. In any case, the bulk of the Russell Hotel didn't afford them protection for very long. In March 1944 they were bombed out again. As Jeannette reported a few days later: "Luckily we left [London] when we did last Tuesday as an incendiary got my bedroom and missed my bed by 2ft. Place is uninhabitable at the moment."

Towards the end of the war, Tawney had to go to London for a meeting of the University Grants Commission. Normally they would have paid for first-class fares and taxis, but neither was available. "So Henry had to walk, leaving here at 7am on foot and when he walked he crossed some fields to save time and got drenched and then had to sit on the floor of the [train] corridor. The travelling has become very severe on this line."

Post-war years

February 1947: "Henry had to go back when term began, so I have been down here with only a sheepdog for company and the stillness of the snow. It is rather like living in a mountain hut because no cars come and there is no traffic or sound… Returning from London, our taxi took the upper road, thinking it could bring us to within a few minutes of our cottage. But alas it stuck in the snow and ice and we had to walk. I proudly managed to carry two bottles of beer, which was an achievement. Here we have coal and wood and paraffin, which is remarkable as there have been no deliveries of late of paraffin and in London it is quite unobtainable."

Harvesting on a summer's day - and the superb view from the hamlet stretching down the valley and 15 miles along the Cotswold escarpment, with hardly a building in sight

The snow was deep that winter, with drifts as high as the stone walls in some places. And it lasted well into March, when the thaw brought flooding.

Later that year, the Tawneys lost the third member of their family, the sheepdog Bob. Not having children of their own, they were perhaps more than usually attached to him. Jeannette told William: "We have had the sorrow of putting our old dog to sleep and miss him dreadfully. He had a stroke and both his back legs were paralysed."

The next big event in Elcombe was the arrival of electricity. In 1951, Jeannette reported: "There is a rumour now that electricity is to be brought up the lane in the following six months. It would be a great advantage to have it as the lamps Tilley, though satisfactory, cannot be turned on again to read in bed which is Harry's main complaint against them. He has the nightly habit of reading at all hours." In fact, it seems to have taken about two years, but in October 1953 she says: "We find the difference of the coal and electric fire an immense gain and the electric light as we have not to worry about the oil lamps."

There have also been other improvements. "We have had our

On Shanks's pony

Before the 20th century, most Elcombe people did their travelling with their feet. There wasn't much choice, unless you were the family that owned Furners Farm, in which case you'd have had a horse and cart. Early in the 1900s there was a horse-drawn bus from Slad to Stroud, and by the 1920s one or two people had their own motorbikes. In the 1930s, the Tawneys of Rose Cottage were sailing around in their pony and trap, but by then Stan Fletcher at the farm was into a succession of motor-cars. When needed, his car of the moment would serve as the village ambulance.

By the 1990s, most houses had two cars and all had at least one; the Nevilles had a collection (though not all quite roadworthy). For their visits, the Myles's have always come in a camper van, which provides some of the conveniences not available in their cottage. Otherwise, the hamlet has been populated mostly with small saloons — Fiats and Ford Fiestas — with a sprinkling of Volvo Estates, the odd Mercedes at Under Catswood and Michael Court's consecutive string of Porsches.

With the exploding car population, traffic on the lane has increased enormously. Twenty-five years ago, the sound of an approaching car might be enough to make you glance up; there were often only two or three an hour and you'd recognise most of the drivers. Nowadays, it's more like two or three every 10-15 minutes — and you probably don't recognise half of them.

Ponies from a neighbouring field were mobilised, Graham Wenman recounted in his Elcombe Epics, when an old elm tree in Laurie Lee's Wood (Tranter's Hill) fell across the lane one snowy winter's day. It had held up several cars, including the local squire's Rolls Royce, seen in the picture

front wall remade, which gives the cottage a much more attractive appearance... The road above the cottage has improved because there are now many more cars requiring to use it so if you come by Seven Springs to Stancombe you do not have to face a long drive."

Apart from the Sadleirs at Througham, the Wares at Amberley, the headmistress of Westonbirt School and doubtless others of the same social set, Jeannette was also on good terms with some of her more immediate neighbours. She went riding with a Mrs Pat Williams, who in the late '30s had "put up a very plucky effort to make a living for herself by breeding Scotties when her husband went off and left her". (Mrs Williams could perhaps have lived at Catswood Cottage, where Jessica Fitzwilliam later bred corgis.) And she went to at least one party at the Woodcocks', the family then living "on the way up the hill towards Bisley" – at Lypiatt Park.

In the better times, before her health declined seriously, she and Harry often had weekend visitors at the cottage. But Jeannette was never a model housewife. Wherever they lived was a mess, according to Terrill, "not only because Tawney was untidy, but because of her own impulsive, distracted ways." Her sense of dress was odd, to say the least, with "spreading, sprouting second-hand hats that stopped people in the street". And she apparently had an obsession for talking about sex in what Terrill calls 'vivid terms'. To their hostess, the author Pearl Buck, in China, she said: "Your husband – he looks as if he must be a beast in bed. Is he?"

Apart from her letters themselves, probably Jeannette Tawney's most enduring contribution to the history of Elcombe will have been her discovery of the bones of one of the earliest people to have lived and died here (see chapter 1). The find excited her – "it has fired me and made me want to excavate and dig everywhere" – but it seems to have been her only significant venture into palaeontology.

Jeannette's extravagance was the main problem she posed for her husband, however. Her spending outran his purse. Kingsley Martin, the editor of the *New Statesman,* remarked that 'Tawney wrote a book called *The Acquisitive Society*, and Mrs Tawney illustrated it'.

A year after selling Rose Cottage in 1955, Jeannette was in hospital in London. She died in January 1958.

Outside the kitchen door

9 'A FUNNY OLD COCKER'
John Papworth

When Tawney came to leave Elcombe, he decided to sell off a good part of his library. The word reached a London bookseller, Peter Eaton, who numbered among his friends the secretary of the South Kensington Labour Party, a certain John Papworth. Then in his early 30s, Papworth was also an activist in the Campaign for Nuclear Disarmament (CND) and part-time chauffeur to Bertrand Russell, whom he would ferry to CND events.

Peter and John decided to make an excursion to deepest Gloucestershire to have a look at Tawney's books. When they got here, John Papworth decided on a rather bigger investment. By his own account, he promptly fell in love with the place, made Tawney an offer and bought Rose Cottage for £800. So in place of an upper-middle-class intellectual and social reformer, a scruffy professor revered by the highest in the land, Elcombe acquired someone who probably shared many of the same ideals but chose other paths to pursue them. It was never Tawney's style to challenge authority with protest marches, sit-ins or hunger strikes, but all these have been part of Papworth's armoury at one time or another. Seeing human or social rights under threat, he has never been afraid to be confrontational, with the result that he has seen the inside of police stations on several occasions.

One weekend at Elcombe (and for him, like Tawney, the cottage was a retreat from working life in London), John met the philosopher Leopold Kohr, who had bought a cottage just up the valley for the woman in his life, Diana Lodge. It was a meeting of minds, with Papworth finding someone whose critique of the modern world had much in common with his own. Kohr's principal concept was that "wherever something is wrong, something is too big" and he had published his seminal work, *The Breakdown of Nations*, only a few

[73]

years before. Not many of the seeds germinated from that book, however, until E F Schumacher planted them in his 1973 best-seller, *Small is Beautiful*. In the meantime, John Papworth was publishing frequent articles by Kohr in *Resurgence*, the magazine he founded in 1966. When Kohr died in 1994 after a life which had gained him only limited public recognition, one London newspaper published a lengthy obituary, describing him as a leading thinker of the 20th century.

From orphanage to presidential palace

John Papworth did not have the most auspicious start in life. He was brought up in an orphanage, but then taken under the wing of a kind landlady in Earl's Court, where he rented rooms as a student. When she declined the owner's offer to sell her the house for a very modest sum, John bought it instead. He says the Council paid him more than ten times as much when they wanted to demolish the house for a road-widening scheme a few years later.

In the early 1960s, in between his weekends and holidays at Elcombe, another fortuitous meeting had an important impact on the direction of John's life. He was asked if he could help an exiled African politician who needed accommodation – and thus he met Kenneth Kaunda, who soon after was to become President of Zambia when the country gained independence in 1964. The two became friendly and Papworth invited Kaunda to visit him at Rose Cottage. He also arranged to present Kaunda with a Jersey calf as a symbolic gift for the new African nation. The calf was named 'Zambia' and the resultant photograph, taken on the track above Furners Farm, was published in the Stroud News and has become one bit of history familiar to almost everyone in the hamlet. To our knowledge, no Head of State since Charles I has visited Elcombe (and he only passing by on the outskirts), so a Head of State-in-waiting was certainly impressive enough. The story at the time (Papworth's political spin?) was that the calf would be taken to Northern Rhodesia 'to improve the local breed'. Whatever the intention, that did not happen: in the end it was sold at Gloucester market.

But if the calf didn't make it, Papworth did. After Zambia's independence, he was invited to Lusaka in 1970 as Personal Adviser to Kaunda and stayed 10 years. Before that, however, the 1960s had been an eventful decade for him in other ways. Shortly after the

'A FUNNY OLD COCKER' [75]

The calf before the country: political exile Kenneth Kaunda (left) is presented with a calf called Zambia on a visit to Elcombe around 1962 with John Papworth (third from left). Two years later, upon independence, he became the first President of the country of that name. With them, Kaunda's aide, Simon Kapwepwe, and farmer Stan Fletcher

Kaunda photograph, he went off to the USA, Mexico and Cuba as 'Personal Representative of Bertrand Russell' and correspondent for *Peace News*. In the States, he was jailed for associating with a peace march and went on hunger strike for 13 days to protest the treatment of other marchers. Then, in Cuba, he won the heart of a French girl whom Fidel Castro had his eye on. Waiting for an interview with Castro, Papworth was asked, "You don't mind if another journalist comes along?" – and it turned out to be an attractive young French woman, Marcelle Fouquet, who was then working at the French Cultural Mission in New York. Afterwards, Castro made a date with her at Havana's grandest hotel, but Marcelle kept him at arm's length. "She was the most beautiful girl I had ever set eyes on", says John, and they were married the same year in Zambia, with President Kaunda as best man.

Ordained as a priest in middle life, John Papworth seemed to take holy orders as a justification for going where most Anglican angels fear to tread. Over the years he has campaigned against war, against the fluoridation of public water supplies, against the enforced state schooling of his children, against supermarkets and inflated institutions of all kinds that smother the human scale, and most vehemently of all against British subversion by what he calls 'the europlot' – the European Community. Recently he was prosecuted and fined £70 for refusing to participate in the UK Census. In his defence, he declared: "If I were to fill in the Census form I would be increasing the power of the government, and government today is using its power to promote mischief, sedition and treason."

A spy in the ointment

Whereas Jeannette Tawney had been suspected of 'harbouring spies' at Rose Cottage due to lights seen in her garden during the wartime blackout, Papworth did actually harbour a notorious Russian spy – though not at Elcombe, and, he insists, quite unintentionally. As with Kaunda, Papworth sometimes allowed bona fide political refugees or others to stay in his Earl's Court flat, and when a fellow peace campaigner rang him at the cottage in 1966 to ask for a bed for someone in need, he agreed. It was only when he got back to London a few days later, he asserts, that he realised who his house guest was: none other than the escaped Soviet spy George Blake, then the object of an intense police hunt. Papworth saw enough of Blake to form a very negative impression of him, but he didn't turn him in either. Blake was soon moved to another safe house before being smuggled off to Moscow.

Every Friday, when he arrived at the cottage, Papworth would walk down to Furners Farm to buy his eggs and milk. He would also use a yoke to get water from the spring, especially after lifting the lid of the Tawneys' rainwater tank and finding a dead rat floating in it. For some time, he rented the field in front of the cottage to Brian Cooper of The Vatch, who kept 300 rabbits there. The field – later turned into a parking lot – used to be known as 'The Vineyard', though Papworth said he could hardly imagine it producing a worthwhile grape harvest.

Cooper remembers the time he went up to ask if he could have use of the land. Papworth, who was outside, told him to wait while he went indoors for pen and paper to write 'a proper lease'. "I thought,

'Uh-uh, here we go'," recalls Cooper, expecting that this meant Papworth would want a proper rent. But when he came out, the lease he'd scribbled was for one shilling a year. So what kind of person was the owner of Rose Cottage in his view? "Oh, a funny old cocker," said Cooper, with a twinkle in his eye. Eventually, he gave up the land when he found it too much to walk up at 6am to feed the rabbits before going to his job in Stroud.

"The Rev John Papworth," said the caption to this portrait across five columns of The Guardian in 1997, "who believes the effect of giant stores on local shops and communities justifies shoplifting"

When John and Marcelle returned from Zambia around 1980, it was with three children who had all been born there: Pierre, John-David and Marie. No doubt for them rural Gloucestershire was something of a culture shock and to begin with the other Elcombe children found them 'a bit strange'. But before they had a chance to become part of the 'gang' of Clarkes, Nevilles and Sharps, the Papworths decided to sell. As John explained later, trying to live in two places just didn't work, so Abercorn Place, St Johns Wood, became the family home for the next 13 years until Marcelle's death in 1995.

Burial on Dunkite Hill

When he sold the cottage, however, John Papworth kept two acres of the Dunkite Hill woodland at the top of the garden behind the house. It was there that traveller Gerry Vaughan later found a convenient place for his decrepit caravan, with an access track from the lane above the hairpin bend and no one to disturb him except a few badgers. And on Marcelle's death, the family decided to bury her there on the top of the hill, almost in the shadow of Gerry's famously under-functioning windmill.

The interment followed a Requiem Mass the previous day in London, celebrated by the Bishop of Fulham with composer John Tavener playing the organ. The burial ceremony was a moving and probably unique occasion, with a Church of England clergyman officiating at the burial of his wife on unconsecrated ground in the middle of a beech wood with about 50 family, friends and former Elcombe neighbours in attendance. Diana Lodge's son, Colin, the stepson of Leopold

A one-man protest in Abbey Road, London, on a pedestrian crossing previously made famous by The Beatles

Kohr, was one of those who the previous night had dug the grave. It had been a hard task: they had to cut through a considerable depth of Cotswold stone.

About 20 people waited around Gerry's caravan for the main party to arrive. At a certain moment a small, yellow tradesman's van appeared, and it was not until its rear doors were opened that we realised this was the hearse. The coffin was carried in procession through the trees to the highest point of the hill. As everyone gathered round, John said some prayers and then invited anyone to speak of their memories of Marcelle. Several did, and one or two others read poems. Then people sat down and listened to some music played on the flute. After more prayers, flowers were laid on the coffin, which was then lowered. One of the Papworths' sons and a friend took spades and filled in the grave, and the service concluded with the singing of 'Jerusalem'. Most people then made their way to Diana Lodge's home at Trillgate, including Gerry with his violin.

The Church disapproves

Two years later, now aged 75, the maverick Papworth was making headlines as 'The Shoplifting Vicar' after he told a crime prevention meeting, at which some senior police officers were present, that pinching goods on display in supermarkets was not a bad thing. *The Guardian*, which interviewed him and ran a story across five columns, described him as "a veteran campaigner against huge supermarkets, which he believes are destroying community life and putting temptation in the way of people who cannot afford their goods". The newspaper quoted him as saying: "I would have no compunction about taking things from giant stores without paying for them. It is not stealing. It is a reallocation of resources which is badly needed. I wouldn't encourage people to go shoplifting, but I think it is perfectly justifiable if they do."

That view of morality was promptly disowned by the Bishop of London and led to Papworth being debarred from preaching at his church in St Johns Wood. But he was unrepentant. "They used to say that silence is golden," he told *The Guardian*, "but now I think it is just yellow."

The following year, John Papworth sold the house in Abercorn Place and moved to a rambling farmhouse in the village of Purton, just outside Swindon. There he continued to produce his campaigning journal, *Fourth World Review*, which he had founded 20 years earlier after failing to regain the editorship of *Resurgence* on his return from Zambia. The *FWR*, appearing five times a year, is sub-titled "For Small Nations, Small Communities, Small Farms, Small Shops, Small Industries, Small Banks, Small Fisheries and the Inalienable Sovereignty of the Human Spirit".

10 Around the houses
The cottages and the people

While Elcombe can be proud of having had in its midst people of strong and admirable principles like Tawney and Papworth, most of the hamlet's history has not been about important people or important events. Until the last 50 years, it has been a history of modest people with limited education and very limited opportunities in life, making what they could of the circumstances they found themselves born into. And since then, their middle-class successors, despite the benefit of much wider horizons and far more opportunity to question the pattern of life laid out for them, have mostly been likewise inclined to accept the world as they found it.

All that history, then, is locked in the little huddle of cottages where anything upto 30 generations have made their homes. Until recent times, they weren't the kind of folk to leave diaries or letters; indeed, until the last hundred years, probably few could read or write. So we can only imagine what life might have been like for those who were here before us, two or three hundred years ago – perhaps when we are trudging up The Pitch in the rain, or standing on the grassy hump at the top of Furner's Farm track on a sunny summer evening.

About the houses in the valley, John Papworth has a thing or two to say in his 'Rural Notebook'. The old farmhouses he describes as spacious and dignified, and the cottages – many of them dating back to the settlement of Huguenot weavers – "have a charm and seemliness I have seen nowhere in modern building." Writing in 1969, he went on: "Forty years ago, the main village, the other side of the valley from our hamlet, could not have had more than two dozen or so houses, with a few scattered farms. Now their numbers have more than trebled and the newer ones are easily distinguishable by what one can only call their meanness." In particular, a pair of newish but drab-looking bungalows had come to be called 'the ladies' and 'the gents'.

[81]

Despite a couple of prominent exceptions and some other imperfect but less visible add-ons, Elcombe has retained most of the harmony and sense of proportion given to it by its original builders. And it avoided the post-World War II wave of cheap and cheerless, public convenience house-building that disfigured so many other communities apart from Slad.

Records of the individual cottages and their owners or occupants are for the most part sketchy. The oldest house deeds found in the course of research for this book date from the 1760s (Elcombe Cottage). The Census of 1851 is a helpful record of who was living here at that time, but the rest is essentially anecdotal. Nevertheless, the following 'tour' around the houses is a chance to meet some colourful characters such as 'Old Will' King, Lottie Fletcher, Wally Bishop and those of a more recent generation such as architect and boat-builder Graham Wenman and artist Sir Oliver Heywood. We will start at the top with Rose Cottage and wend our way downwards to Woodside by the spring at the bottom.

Rose Cottage

The land behind Rose Cottage and Hillside was sold off in small plots when the common land of Dunkite Hill Wood was enclosed in the 1860s. Either then or later, Rose Cottage acquired two acres or more of woodland along the brow of the hill, also accessible by a track above the hairpin bend.

In the early years of the 20th century, the cottage was owned by William Miles, a shoemaker who had a shop of his own in Threadneedle Street, Stroud. Fifty years later an old-timer remembered that "he made good shoes". There is a picture of Rose Cottage in *Stroud and the Five Valleys in Old Photographs* (2nd Selection, p52), believed by the compilers to have been taken in the 1920s, but the people in it are not identified. All one can say is that somebody was taking good care of the garden. No further information is available on Miles or any other owners until the Tawneys arrived in 1928.

Graham Wenman remembered Tawney out walking in Norfolk jacket and boots, talking to anyone who wanted to chat. He had 'rather strange ways'. Tawney kept the cottage for 27 years before selling to John Papworth, who stayed almost as long, until 1981. Both in their turn went back to London.

Of Tawney's two booksheds, at the top of the garden on the fringe of the wood, the one that survives is still clearly visible from across the valley in Slad. Although he often collected water from the spring with the yoke, he and Jeannette also employed Lou Hanks from The Vatch as an odd-job man, who did it for them.

Janet Bartlett remembers that Tawney kept his trap in a 'coach house' (in reality probably a simple shed) just above the hairpin bend. "If ever Mr Tawney used to see my mother or Mrs Bodenham woodin', or any of us children, he always used to help us with a bundle of wood."

John Papworth added a new living-room to the cottage. Like his predecessor, he was away a lot of the time, either in London editing the magazine *Resurgence*, which he founded in 1966, or in Zambia, where he spent 10 years as Adviser to the President, Kenneth Kaunda.

In 1981, the Papworths sold to an ex-colonial couple, Charles and Margaret Adams, who until recently had been running a country club near Malmesbury. But they soon moved on and the cottage was bought by painter and baronet Oliver Heywood and his wife Denise (Sneeze), coming the short distance from Wick Street, just over the hill in Painswick Valley. The Heywoods turned the paddock into a large parking area and built a studio cabin in the garden, where he held biennial exhibitions of his work, consisting mostly of landscapes from Scotland to Greece, including quite a few in and around Slad. Although essentially figurative, Oliver Heywood's paintings developed an optic from which the viewer seemed to be seeing the scene with several eyes, and in different lights, at the same time. In 1985 he was commissioned to paint a 27-foot long, 12-foot high mural on the west wall of Nailsworth Parish Church, reflecting the life and people of the town. It is an impressive piece of work.

ELCOMBE - Offers over £149,500 - Idyllically situated detached cottage with wonderful panoramic Slad Valley views - huge garden, parking. PLUS detached studio/bungalow in grounds. Ideal for artists etc. PHONE FOR MORE DETAILS.

Rose Cottage, as advertised for sale in 1995. Understandably, perhaps, 'idyllic' is a favourite adjective for Elcombe in the thesaurus of estate agents

Sir Oliver Heywood's title derived from a forebear who was MP for Manchester in the 1830s and who was credited with many good works. After taking part in the Normandy landings in 1944, Oliver met and married Denise when peace came the following year. Though without formal training, he determined to be a painter and in 1947 they moved to a large, 16th century house in Wick Street, where they stayed for 35 years. Then, their three sons having married and left home, they wanted somewhere smaller and bought Rose Cottage.

The Heywoods, along with the Coopers of Furners Farm, were members of a meditation group following The Way of Contemplative

Being. For a period in the 1990s they met on Wednesday evenings and twice on Sundays at the Heywoods' studio. A motto on one of their meeting notices bore the legend:

> 'bound in silence
> discovering
> boundless light and love'

It was while dancing with this group to celebrate the birth of a friend's grandchild that Sir Oliver collapsed and died in 1992. Denise stayed on in Elcombe for a while, but then moved to Stroud. Michael and Diana Carey, experienced counsellors with a grown-up family, became the new owners of Rose Cottage.

Sneeze up a tree

The dowager Lady Heywood, affectionately known as Sneeze, was driving into Stroud in August 1995 when – at a point where there is a row of stout trees just behind the railings on the valley side – her car mounted the pavement, climbed the railings and ended with its nose stuck in the branches of one tree. Being several feet off the ground, she was helped out by some neighbours. Her first remark to them, reportedly, was "Oh hello, isn't it a lovely day?" She got a lift home from Nick Neville, who happened to be passing. Sneeze was none the worse for wear, though in view of her 74 years a bit anxious that the authorities might ask questions about her driving skills.

Hillside

The earliest deeds of Hillside show that it belonged to a John Whiting from 1824-54, overlapping briefly with the Thomas Whiting who was at Yew Tree Cottage until 1827. The Whitings were a numerous family in the district, but it's just possible that this was the same John Whiting who was listed in a Bisley document of 1809 as "a Protestant dissenter".

In the 1860s, ownership passed to John Bartlett (see Chapter 5), probably when he bought one of the plots sold off in the Bisley enclosures. On his death in 1875, four years after taking over Furners Farm, Bartlett bequeathed Hillside to a Stroud grocer, William Sims, who was an important figure in the town and for many years Chairman of Stroud Urban District Council. Sims had a shop in the High Street, advertising himself as "Grocer and Provision Merchant" and selling "British Wines". From Sims the cottage passed to a builder, William Skinner, in 1893, then to a Mary Eliza Pegler, who in 1906 sold it to a Stroud policeman, Sam Spicer. But it's unlikely any of them lived here; for many years before this date, the cottage was rented to a Rachel Tyler and latterly to George Eyers, who worked for the Council on road maintenance around Slad. George's grandson, Jack Eyers, also lived in Elcombe for a time (see Kenwood Cottage below), and when Bill Tuck got too old to use them, he gave Jack – also a builder – all his stone-cutting tools.

Deeds of the early 1900s record that the cottage was bounded on one side by the road and on the others mostly by land of William Miles (Rose Cottage) and the Dorringtons of Lypiatt Park, who had bought several lots at the time of the enclosures a few decades earlier.

In 1915, the house was tenanted by Arthur Brown, his wife Gertrude and six children, who stayed until 1921 before moving to Bisley. The house changed hands twice while they were there – first when Police Constable Sam Spicer sold to another member of his family, then when it was bought by Mrs Florence Stratford, wife of Albert Stratford, mechanic.

The Browns had five sons and one daughter. Their second son, Leslie (b.1905), recalled coming to Elcombe at the age of 10 when the family moved back from Wales. His grandfather had previously lived in Slad. His father was a decorator and Leslie took up the trade on leaving school at 13. Until then he walked to Slad School across the fields, often accompanied by Molly, one of the five children of their neighbour, 'Butcher' Pole (Woodside). A Mr Hewison – tenant or owner of Furners Farm before Fletcher Snr acquired it in 1919 – had a bull in the field, but it had a chain from its horns to a piece of wood across its forelegs, so it couldn't chase him.

Les Brown said he was on the small side compared with other boys his age, but he was tough. When his younger brother was attacked by another boy, Les beat up the assailant. The boy's older brother then waylaid him after school, but Les – with his hob-nailed boots – dealt with him, too. "I rolled up my sleeves. It was a very wet night and the girls were standing round in a circle. When the boy's mother brought him up to Elcombe afterwards to show my mother his injuries and to protest, my mother said it served him right."

Shocking short skirts

Les's elder brother, Jack, who was friendly with Gwen Fern of Yew Tree Cottage, later married a girl from Nottingham, who disgusted the village with her short skirts. Sometimes they were above the knee, which was unheard of in country areas. Les married in 1925 and lived in the same house in Bisley from 1931 until his death in 1998. In 1928, after moving to Bisley, he worked on the renovation of Owlpen Manor for leading Arts & Crafts architect, Norman Jewson. Les is seen in a group photo taken at Owlpen at that time and published in Juliet Shipman's *Bisley*. He stayed 22 years in the decorating trade, worked briefly for a bomb-making factory in WWII, then with Danarm for 30 years till his retirement in 1970. By 1995, aged 90, he had nine grandchildren, eight great grandchildren, with a great-great-grandchild on the way. He'd had a big party when he was in hospital earlier in the year on his 90th birthday.

After 1920, the Stratfords kept the house for 34 years. Jimmy Stratford worked for Smith & Lee, the hardware store in Stroud; they had a son, Bernard, and daughter, Sissy. Then, in 1954, they sold to a Mrs Dorothea Enthoven, described by Graham Wenman as "an unusual, rather arty person, living on her own." John Papworth was less charitable about her lifestyle after finding her once in her dressing-gown in the middle of the day eating cornflakes over her stove. Mrs Enthoven was divorced, but she had a nephew and niece, Bill and Clare, who sometimes stayed with her in school holidays. She did a bit of dressmaking to make ends meet. Clare remembers that her aunt was very eccentric; as children they had a good time in the country, but the house was "in frightful condition".

Mrs Enthoven stayed until 1962 and then sold to a Sydney and Lilian Howarth from Birmingham. But Mrs Howarth didn't like the place and reputedly never lived there, though latterly they started some renovation – digging the back of the cottage out of the hillside. The Howarths had paid £880 for the house, but they got £17,500 when they passed it on to fireman Nick Neville, his wife Ann and their family 16 years later. Somewhere along the line, the cottage – which had originally been called Fort View, presumably because one could see across to Rodborough Fort on the other side of Stroud – had its name changed to Hillside.

Asked about it later, Nick Neville said he knew there used to be an old quarry at the bottom of the hairpin bend. But he didn't know it was the place where Jeannette Tawney had found the neolithic bones, and he had largely filled it in with rubble when building an extension to the cottage.

AROUND THE HOUSES

Under Catswood

Dunkite Hill was common land until the 1860s, when it was bought by the Dorringtons of Lypiatt Park under the Bisley Enclosure Award. Sometime after World War II, ten acres of it were bought by Caleb Tuck – son of Bill Tuck (Woodside Cottage) – who was by then apparently doing quite well in the haulage business. Caleb wanted to build six pairs of semi-detached cottages, but when that was blocked he got planning permission for a single house on the grounds that he needed to be near his elderly parents. In fact, he then sold the land to Rosie Bailey, who was a potter and had been at the University of Reading. She had a pretty cottage at Tunley, a hamlet on the way from Bisley to Cirencester, and John Papworth says it was he who introduced her to Elcombe.

High on the hillside, overlooking the little knot of traditional Cotswold stone cottages which is most of Elcombe, Rosie Bailey proceeded in 1967 to build an uncompromisingly modern, single-storey house with picture windows to make the most of the spectacular view. Some people wondered how she managed to get permission for a building in such contrast to the rest of the hamlet.

The house that Rosie built - a daring newcomer of the 1960s, but set enough apart that it did not clash with the architectonic unity of the main cluster of cottages

Be that as it may, Rosie had many artistic friends, among them Marian Francis, who was something of a sculptress and who came to Elcombe in the 1960s (Yew Tree Cottage). One of Rosie's admirers – a well-known stone carver, Simon Verity – carved a stone with her name and a heart on it, which is still built into the wall forming the property's southern boundary.

After Rosie, in 1972, came Victor and Jane Roffe: he a prosperous, retired carpet dealer from London, who had met Jane, then a nurse, when he was in hospital. They were sometimes away on long-distance travels, but when in residence Jane interspersed her golf with bell-ringing at Painswick Church and feeding the foxes that frequented her lawn. It was the Roffes who gave Under Catswood its name, taking up someone's suggestion that they vary Dylan Thomas's "Under Milk Wood".

In the early '90s, the Roffes decided to move to warmer climes and bought themselves a flat in Monte Carlo. They were succeeded by Peter and Joan Shillito, Peter having recently retired from his legal practice in Cheltenham.

The gypsy caravan

There was a splendid gypsy caravan in Elcombe for several decades. A gaily-painted, traditional wagon, it had some ornate glass panels inside and everything but the old nag to pull it. The caravan first arrived in the 1960s when a friend of Diana Lodge and Leopold Kohr asked the then owner of Rose Cottage, John Papworth, if she could park it on the land in front of his house. Papworth agreed and this "very arty, very dashing middle-aged lady"– whose name he couldn't remember – spent some time living there with her daughter. As well as lacking water, the caravan must have been a bit draughty: "They were always coming to me for water and warmth." But then they packed up to go to Australia and sold the four-wheeler to the Roffes of Under Catswood, where for quite a few years it graced their drive. Being at that point in need of refurbishment, they restored it to sparkling condition and allowed some of the Elcombe children to play and sleep in it overnight. But the caravan's owners seemed destined to have itchy feet and in the end the Roffes migrated to Monte Carlo. The caravan found a new home for some years at Fletcher's Knapp until eventually sold and taken away.

Yew Tree Cottage

The first recorded owner of Yew Tree Cottage was a Thomas Whiting, whose deed of sale in 1827 still exists. We don't know how long he had been there, but he sold it for £15 to 'Rachel Gregory of Ferners'. And presumably like many in the village he was illiterate, since he signed the deed with an 'X'.

The Whitings had been in Bisley a long time. In 1572, a 'John Whitinge of Bisleye' is recorded as having received a bequest from someone's will. By 1831, seven Whitings owned 23 houses in Bisley between them. Conceivably ours was the same Thomas Whiting who at that date was renting a house and garden in Bisley with a rateable value of £3. This would have been a fairly decent house, given that the cheapest ones were rated at 15 shillings and farmhouses at £5-8.

Rachel Gregory was already a widow, so she could just have been the same Rachel Gregory who in 1783 witnessed the will of a certain Timothy Rotten, in which he left his 'messuage' to the Bisley baker, Thomas Gregory (presumably her relative) in payment of his debts. In any event, she rented out Yew Tree Cottage, possibly to agricultural labourers working for her at Furners Farm. When she bought the cottage, it was described as "bounded on the east by the garden of Sarah Tranter [Habricia Cottage?], on the south by the gardens and premises of Mary Wright, Thomas Snow and Thomas King [Elcombe Cottages], on the west by the garden of William Fletcher and on the north by the common [Dunkite Hill]."

Rachel Gregory died intestate, so the cottage passed to her daughter, Sophia Selwyn, widow of Daniel, who did the same in 1867. The next four owners, from 1869 to 1925, were a plasterer, two bakers and a carpenter – all of them buy-to-let landlords. Tenants before the turn of the century included Isaac Hitchings and George Russell, but there is no information about any of them to hand. Carpenter Albert Jones, who bought the place in 1896 for £50, rented it sometime before 1908 to Arthur Fern and his wife, Maud, because that is the year their daughter, Gwendoline, was born there. A son, William, followed in 1912, but with the outbreak of World War I, Arthur Fern joined up as a Private in the Somerset Light Infantry. He was later killed in France.

Arthur Fern's young widow, Maud, then married his brother, Ernest, who took over the lease of the cottage. They had a daughter of their own, Dorothy. Ernest was a postman and he rose to become Assistant

Mrs Maud Fern, mistress of Yew Tree Cottage for more than 30 years.

Postmaster at Stroud Post Office. In 1925 he bought the cottage for £100 and the family stayed there until the start of World War II. According to his step-daughter, Ernest Fern was a very keen gardener and would stay out in all weathers, often ignoring his wife's pleas to come in.

Bill Fern, born at Yew Tree Cottage in 1912, followed his step-father into the Post Office, first as messenger boy and then as postman serving Chalford and Stroud. Resplendent in his uniform with peaked cap and badge, he appears with six colleagues in a group photograph of the Chalford P.O. staff in 1935 (*Stroud in Old Photographs*, 2nd Collection, p145). Bill Fern received the Imperial Service Medal and retired at 60 after 46 years service broken only by six years in the army during World War II. He married in 1941 and set up home in Bisley Rd, Stroud. He died in 1998 aged 86.

Longest memories

In the mid-1980s, Gwen and William Fern were certainly two of the oldest (if not the oldest) surviving people born in Elcombe. William remembered that his mother used to walk into Stroud with a pram, either to carry the kids or the shopping. The only public transport from Slad was a horse and cart on Tuesday and Friday run by a farmer from Sheepscombe. The fare to Stroud was two pence. Paraffin for the cottage's Aladdin lamps was bought from the Slad Post Office and William recalled carrying the one-gallon cans up the hill. As a child he sometimes took fledgling jays and magpies from their nests and reared them tame, even if "they weren't so good for the garden". He was given pigeons by his friend Wilson Twinning at The Vatch. And at

Christmas time he was one of a group of children from Elcombe and The Vatch who went carol-singing up and down the valley. In his teens he would go to the Star Inn to buy whisky for his uncle, who had come back from working in Canada. A bottle of whisky cost 12s 6d.

The Ferns kept pigs and home-cured the bacon with salt petre and hung it in the wash-house (now the kitchen) which they had built onto the two-up, two-down cottage. Apart from this meat, the garden meant that they were "completely self-supporting in vegetables". Their pig sties were in what is now a woodshed at the end of the house – and William, like everyone else, carried up water for them from the spring in two buckets on a yoke. On one day not to be forgotten he hauled up 20 buckets. The spring also fed a splendid bed of watercress in the field below, just across the road, and he often used to gather it. "It made a splendid dinner with some cheese and bread".

The six-foot long, four-foot high recess under the stairs at the back of Yew Tree's living room was used by the Ferns as a coal store and for keeping cool meat and fish. Gwen's half-sister, Dorothy, remembers seeing mackerel glistening there in the dark and being fascinated by their silver sheen.

There was also a family connection between the Ferns and Carrie Wynn, who farmed at The Camp, a small hamlet on the other side of Bisley. Carrie brought up three children of their cousin Beryl, who had committed suicide, and Beryl's grandmother, another Mrs Wynn, lived at the Riflemans. Carrie was also related to Mrs Vick.

White-collar landlords

After the Ferns, the cottage reverted to being a rental investment for most of the next 20 years – but this time with a new kind of educated, middle-class owner. From 1943 to 1960, it belonged to a teacher from Oxford, Dr Walter Parker-Harrison and his wife. They and their three children are said to have been keen on gardening, though they only occupied it intermittently between tenants. The first to rent it from them were the Bodenhams, a poor family with several unruly children who became somewhat notorious in the neighbourhood. Mr Bodenham worked for the Council and was very kind when sober but often on the drink, when he could be nasty and pick fights with Mr Green or anyone. Bodenham's wife, Dora, was described by a neighbour of the time as 'a rough sort'; her children were in rags but she sold their ration cards outside Woolworths. According to Iris Green, she never had meals ready and "produced a baby every year – eight or nine altogether." The children were really hungry, so perhaps not surprisingly they took to pinching food from other houses...despite which they all turned out well. One of them, Godfrey, was "a very nice boy", Iris Green remembered.

Graham Bodenham, interviewed in 1994, said he was one of nine children. His father used to bicycle every day to his job at Frampton on Severn, until he found work closer to home at Stroud Breweries. Graham remembered having great times in the woods, including hunting for owl's nests in old trees. His family kept two goats and all the garden was planted to vegetables. The bath in the wash-house had a wooden lid to serve as a table. There was an old black kitchen range but of course no running water or electricity. He remembered having long chats with Prof. Tawney.

Cornflakes for the dogs
When the Bodenhams left, the next occupants, from about 1954, were the Hewitt family. They had four daughters, one or more of whom caught the eye of the local lads, but their father was away a lot and his occupation was a mystery. When one of the lads asked, they said, "We don't talk about it," leaving the suspicion that he had been in prison. In the end, the family is said to have done a 'midnight flit', owing rent. Mrs Evie Wenman thought them "a very nice family", but John Papworth had some reservations. Apart from the children, they had "a most uncommon variety of household pets, including a tortoise, several birds in cages, mice, cats galore and two fragile-looking whippets." Passing Mrs Hewitt on the lane one day, he thought the two whippets with her appeared very emaciated and asked whether they didn't need some food. "Oh, I gives 'em their cornflakes and milk regular every morning," she replied. What a wretched diet for a dog, Papworth thought to himself. And when a leg of lamb disappeared from his kitchen just before he was to cook it, the Hewitts – or their hungry whippets – seemed the most likely culprits.

In his Rural Notebook, Papworth says that Hewitt was a semi-invalid on public assistance "and there was no other money coming in". One by one, the local trades people stopped supplying them as the debts mounted up. He goes on: "I had become very fond of three of their cats who got to know me and waited for me to arrive on Fridays.

In the depths of winter I might reach the hamlet after midnight and they would be bunched up on an old fuel bunker outside my scullery window waiting for some supper. They were half wild at first and would spit and scratch if I tried to stroke them, but gradually they grew to accept me and even got to entering the cottage to drink milk whilst I stroked them. I found it hard when I learned the good lady had had them put down when she moved."

Goodbye to all that

Despite its idyllic setting, the inhabitants of the cottage in this period – or any previous period – were not blessed with comfortable, let alone idyllic, lives. Next came Wally Bishop, who in 1960 was retiring after farming for many years at Worgan's Farm just across the valley. He quit the farm soon after his brother drowned there in a well. According to one of his neighbours of the time, Wally drank too much but had been kept in check by his brother. He liked Yew Tree Cottage because he could still see his old fields, using binoculars – but he had only been there two years when life became insupportable. Whether it was the drink, or debt and depression, as some suspected, or the headaches he suffered from a World War I head wound, we do not know. His job in the army had been to train horses that were to be sent to the front, and he had a metal plate where one of them had kicked him in the head. Whatever the cause, he wrote a note to his sister asking her to feed his chickens, then placed a bucket of water on the wall of the cottage terrace and held his head in it until he drowned. John Papworth described Wally Bishop as a lonely man, who liked company very much but drove it away by always conversing at the top of his voice.

After his sad demise, the cottage was bought in 1964 by Dr Hugh and Marian Francis. Dr Francis was a consultant radiologist at Paddington General Hospital, according to Dr John Myles,

Wally Bishop with one of his horses

Yew Tree Cottage - in 1939 and after the conversion of 1985

who was an orthopaedic registrar there at the time and recalls seeing him in the staff dining room. As recalled by Josephine Stroud (Kenwood Cottage), who knew them, Hugh was a doctor who had really wanted to be a painter, and his wife was something of a sculptress. He served a prison sentence for having carried out an abortion and may have been temporarily struck off the medical register, though after retirement he worked as an anaesthetist at Gloucester Royal. "He had a lot of white hair and a long white beard," one neighbour recalls, and he was always a non-conformist in the medical profession as well as having strong left-wing views. He once engaged in a heated argument with a colonel from Knapp House who came seeking election support for the Tories.

During their time at Elcombe, the Francises invited numerous people from the art world as guests. One of the best known of these was the sculptress Elisabeth Frink. Marian Francis was also a keen and knowledgeable gardener and brought back many unusual plants from travels abroad. After her husband's death in 1974, however, she found the maintenance of the steeply terraced garden too much and two years later she decided to move to a more manageable place on the south coast.

(Someone who knew the Francises later told another person in the hamlet that Hugh was actually the son of a wealthy Sri Lankan family. This person, who had visited the family in Colombo, said that both his parents were Ceylonese, but the present author has no information to verify this.)

Next came the author, his Italian wife, Cicci, and their children Leonora and Fabian, then 6 and 3. The moving-in itself was memorable. Standing at the kitchen window on the appointed morning, 10 days before Christmas, waiting for the furniture van to arrive with all our essentials from London, I was looking out over a snowy landscape and wondering if he'd make it. Then, soon after 9am, the big van hove into sight. Having realised in advance that this behemoth could not possibly negotiate the bridle way, a transit van had been hired locally to ferry small loads up from a parking place near the spring. All was anticipation as the first load of beds and basic kitchen stuff began the last 300 yards of their 100-mile journey. But before it reached the half-way mark, the wheels of the transit were spinning on the ice. It slid to a halt and nothing would get it up the last few yards of the hill. So everything had to go back in the big van, which retreated to Brimscombe to wait for the thaw. Fortunately, this came about four days later, so we were installed just in time for Christmas. It was the first of numerous Elcombe adventures in the snow, which later included driving Leonora back from school at Westonbirt in a nil-visibility blizzard.

Upto 1998, Yew Tree Cottage had had 13 owners in 170 years. The first one, Rachel Gregory, kept it the longest – 42 years – but the average has been 13 years apiece. One little mystery concerns the derelict cottage at the bottom of the garden on a small piece of land bought from Mr Myles of Elcombe Cottage in the 1940s. Some say it was once the village bakery, and certainly it does have the remains of a bread oven in one wall, but no documentary evidence has been found.

Lunch at Christmas time (1980s) on the terrace of Yew Tree Cottage

'An unlabelled can of beans'

Anyone taking a walk through Redding Wood in 1982 would have come across a very different kind of caravan from the proud but superannuated gypsy model on display further down the hill. This one was more modern but more scruffy and evidently occupied, with an old Landrover parked nearby. It was the first most people knew that we had a newcomer to the village – an independent traveller dedicated to a simple lifestyle free from the constraints of regular society and the money economy.

The following year, when Redding Wood was sold, Gerry Vaughan had to move – and he found an ideal spot in the woods on the other side of the lane just above the hairpin bend. This was on land that John Papworth had kept when he sold Rose Cottage, so there was no landlord around to complain or disturb him. Over the next few years, Gerry became an acknowledged member of the Elcombe community and was invited to the occasional social gatherings, where he would sometimes contribute to the musical entertainment by playing tunes on his fiddle.

The youngest of five children, Gerry rather followed in the footsteps of his father, who was a maker and repairer of radiograms and other electrical equipment. He loved inventing things. He devised a system for re-circulating

hot air from his motorbike engine to keep his legs warm, and another for distributing heat from the stove in his caravan to warm his bed. But his grand project was the windmill, which was designed to provide him with a source of electricity. After studying many manuals and collecting much scrap iron, it was built and finally erected on the highest point of the land around him. Facing west into the prevailing wind on a bare hill, Gerry might conceivably have illuminated his life with several hundred watts. Only unfortunately it wasn't a bare hill, and the trees all around were considerably taller than the windmill. It seldom if ever generated enough to light a single bulb.

Gerry would regale his neighbours with stories of the electrical repair shop in town which objected when he went rummaging in their skip to recover repairable equipment that they had thrown away. He had found a drill, a circular saw and other things there with only 'minor' defects. "But they don't know I've done five years' apprenticeship in this stuff and had experience after that," he would say. "As far as they're concerned, I'm just an unlabelled can of beans."

Gerry stayed in Elcombe almost 15 years. Denise Heywood at Rose Cottage let him use her garden shed, where, among other things, he recharged his batteries; and he had his mail sent c/o the Nevilles (Hillside), who would hang up his dole cheques with a clothes peg on the line outside their cottage, so that he could collect them when going to the spring for water.

As a regular user of the spring, he was not surprisingly one of the objectors to Michael Court's fence around it. Whether it was a coincidence or not, within a year of the incident in which he resorted to direct action and tried to chop down the fence with an axe, Gerry decided to move on. He said he was heading for Wales, but he'd barely got down to the bottom of the hill and turned onto the Slad Road when a wheel fell off his caravan.

Gerry at one of the hamlet's Christmas parties

Furners Farm

The farm is probably the oldest existing homestead in Elcombe. The 1976 Victoria History says that "in the extreme west of the [Steanbridge] tithing is the house formerly called King's Place but later called Furners Farm after the family that held it by copy [a form of leasehold] in the 16th century and as a freehold in the 18th." It adds that the farmhouse "retains a traditional plan and is apparently of the 16th century, but it was partly rebuilt and enlarged to the west in the 17th century and again enlarged, to the south, in the late 19th". If correct, this suggests either that the original name of King's Place survived for only a few decades, or that the Furner family demolished a previous house of that name and started again. In the latter case, there may have been a farm on this site at least a hundred years or more earlier, putting it among the oldest in the valley. In any case, the name 'King's Place' is more likely to refer to some member of the local and prolific King family, who had owned land around Bisley since at least the early 1600s, rather than to a monarchical connection.

One 18th century reference to Furners occurs in Bisley's Poor Rate Assessment of 1777 – the tax on householders to defray the cost of services for the sick and the poor. This lists 'Catswood Estate and Furners R: Wm Poulson – 11/9¾d monthly', and also 'House at Furners R: Thos Arndell – 5¼d and 2¾d'. At Catswood, William Poulson was a tenant of the Lypiatt Park Estate, but more research would be needed to establish whether he owned or leased Furners, and which property was occupied by Thomas Arndell.

Moving on 50 years, the next recorded owner or occupier of the farm is 'Rachel Gregory of Ferners', who bought Yew Tree Cottage in 1827 and whose servant signed the deed for her. One can guess that it was intended as a tied cottage for her farm workers, though by the census of 1851 her daughter, Sophia, was installed there. By the same date, the farm had passed to Sarah Mayo, a widow aged 55 with two sons and two daughters. Twenty years later it was in the hands of John and Rachel Bartlett, who with their numerous offspring had previously been occupying one of the tiny Elcombe cottages.

One wonders how John Bartlett, who was still listed as 'Labourer' in his mid-40s, found the means to acquire Furners and its 51 acres, as well as one of the cottages sold off in the enclosures of the 1860s. But somehow he did – and on his death in 1871 he passed it on to two sons-in-law, the brothers Thomas and George Partridge, who had married two of his daughters, Elizabeth and Emma respectively, just a year or two before.

There is not much information to hand about the first years of the 20th century, when farming was going through one of its recurrent crises. For children of the time, one of the memorable things about the farm was a bull, which had a wooden bar across its forelegs to prevent it charging people who crossed its field.

Furners Farm (left) and Fletchers Knapp - detail from a painting by Gwen Wenman, 1968

In 1919 came the Fletchers, who also owned land at Kings Stanley, a few miles on the other side of Stroud, and they kept it for 57 years. For a time it was farmed by Fletcher senior; then, when his son Stan got married, he moved in with his new wife, Lottie. In *Cider with Rosie*, Laurie Lee recalls that when he was in the Infants class at Slad school in the early 1920s, one of the sounds they could hear through the window was "Fletcher's chattering mower".

Stan Fletcher was a quiet man, according to Janet Bartlett, whose father, Frank, worked for Fletcher as cowman almost all his life. And he never carried any cash – or at least claimed not to. Janet worked on the farm at weekends and remembers him telling her frequently: "I haven't any money on me, Jan, I'll pay you next week." But in retrospect, at least, she didn't seem to mind too much. Lottie, on the other hand, Janet described as "a really mean woman". Maybe that was her nature, or maybe there was a bitterness that stemmed from her inability to have children. Lottie had been pregnant once, but she miscarried after being trampled by a cow.

By this time there was tap water at the farm, Janet remembers, because there was a ram in the field that pumped it up. But the Bartletts had no toilet or bath in their cottage. John Myles also remembered the ram:

> "The water ram which supplied Furners Farm made a very distinctive noise. If one walked down through the fields, perhaps to attend the Easter service at Holy Trinity church, which would be decorated with dozens of jam-jars filled with primroses, the noise of the ram would be a quite good guide to the route as the path ran near the ram. (What a brilliant 18th century invention the ram was, too - no power source except the water itself, flowing into a closed dome, compressing the air until, suddenly, there was enough force to drive some water from the base of the dome up the pipe)."

Watering the roses

Whatever her problems, Lottie was evidently something of a dragon – and her meanness showed to others as well. A nephew of hers, K R Mills, who lived with his family in Kent, spent holidays at Furners from about 1932 when he was 10. But he recalls that it was less of a holiday than staying at home! Fletcher made him work hard, and on days when Lottie gave Stan bacon and eggs for breakfast, he only got a crust of bread. Mills was also given the job of gathering plums or nuts, and even if they came to only 1 or 2 lbs they would be taken to Stroud market. Mills thought Lottie didn't care for Professor Tawney because of his reformist ideas of helping the poor – evidently not a priority of hers. Before – and possibly even after – the advent of flush toilets, Lottie would announce a call of nature by declaring to anyone present, "I'm just going to water the roses".

Fletcher's first car – almost certainly the first in Elcombe – was a bull-nosed Morris, Mills recalled. It was followed by an American Terraplane and later a Vauxhall Velox. In emergencies, when someone was injured or seriously ill, it was Fletcher they would turn to – and he would drive them into Stroud hospital. He was also believed to have had the first tractor in the valley, but before that he had two sturdy carthorses called Tommy and Dobbin. The first telephone in the hamlet was also Fletcher's, consisting of a wall-mounted wooden box with the earpiece hanging on a hook on one side and a handle on the other which you turned to call the exchange.

During WWII, when there was no petrol for civilian use, Stan Fletcher took his milk down to Stroud Creamery every morning with a horse-drawn milk float. Some time after the war, John Myles recalls, a large wooden platform was erected at the top of the farm

That sinking feeling (nearly)

Three Elcombe people from Furners Farm escaped with their lives by chance from one of the great disasters of the 20th century. The current owner, Simon Cooper, was visited in the year 2000 by a Canadian lady, Laurie Hitchings, who said she wanted to see the farm because her grandfather had lived there for a period upto about 1914.

Her grandfather, it turns out, was John Thomas Hitchings, who in 1892 had married Edith Sarah Partridge – presumably a daughter of one of the Partridge-Bartlett couples. Quite possibly he was also related to the Daniel Hitchings living at Habricia or Linden Cottage around that time.

In 1911 the Hitchings family decided to explore the possibility of migrating to Canada and finding themselves a farm on the prairies. So, leaving his wife behind to mind Furners for the time being, John and his two sons booked passage on a transatlantic liner of the White Star Line. It was going to be a special trip and the tickets were all paid for.

When they got to Southampton, however, Mr Hitchings was approached on the quayside by a wealthy family desperate to join friends already booked for this particular voyage. According to grand-daughter Laurie, they offered him three times whatever he had paid for his tickets and, with some reluctance, he eventually accepted. He and his sons watched from the pier, with a sense of anti-climax one must suppose, as the ship cast off and steamed away towards the horizon.

The liner was the Titanic.

A year after hearing this story, Simon Cooper was visited by another member of the Hitchings family, who had a slightly more prosaic version (that they were bumped off the liner because it had been overbooked). We prefer the original story, so we're sticking with that.

Anyway, the Hitchings trio were still at Southampton, waiting for a booking on the next available ship, when news of the unsinkable liner's sinking was received. In the end they went, found the kind of place they wanted, and after packing up at Furners the family was reunited on the prairies of Saskatchewan.

track, and the milk churns were placed there for collection by lorry. Two prisoners of war worked at Furners: Paul Hartmann, a German, and John Kunz, a Czech. After the war, Kunz went to work for Stan's brother, Jim, at Kings Stanley, while Hartmann stayed on for a few years at Furners. From the 1930s, Guy Alcock, a doctor's son from Gloucester, was classed as a paying guest with the Fletchers, though he was also expected to work. He'd had meningitis as a child and was rather slow mentally. When Lottie said she couldn't take care of him any more, his father refused to have him back so he was sent to Coney Hill Hospital, a mental institution – but Janet says there was nothing really wrong with him.

In the 1960s, there was some excitement in the valley when plans were being made for a film version of *Cider with Rosie*. The film-makers approached Lottie Fletcher for permission to spray artificial snow on her fields for a winter scene, but she refused.

From pigs to printing

In 1976, after Stan's death, the farm went to auction. The house and eight acres were bought by Jim and Barbara Clarke, who previously lived at Chalford, while the other 40 acres were sold separately. Jim, whose background was in the printing business, aimed to run the

The Clarkes at Furners: Simon, Louise, Barbara and Grandma Yvonne

farm singlehandedly as a small-holding, and before long he had goats, geese, pigs and a cow and was hard at work developing a vegetable plot. Using her two spare rooms, Barbara started a bed-and-breakfast business and gave many visitors — including some from overseas — their first taste of rural Cotswold life. But it proved hard to make a living from the smallholding and before long, working in an outbuilding, Jim started the Slad Valley Press, taking on small print jobs from local businesses and later converting the farm basement into his printing shop. Since it started in 1980, one of Jim's contracts, appropriately enough, was to print the Slad Valley News.

With their children, Simon and Louise, and their lovable chocolate labrador, Henry, who quickly became a village pet, the Clarkes were a pivot of activities in the hamlet. Jim became a member of the Woolpack quiz team, and for a time Barbara was involved in trying to revivify the somewhat moribund Slad Society. They were then joined by Barbara's mother, Yvonne Dunn, a jolly, grandmotherly figure, who first had Springfield Cottage for a time before moving to the farm's own cottage. This the Clarkes had converted from a scruffy outbuilding, initially for some extra b-and-b income.

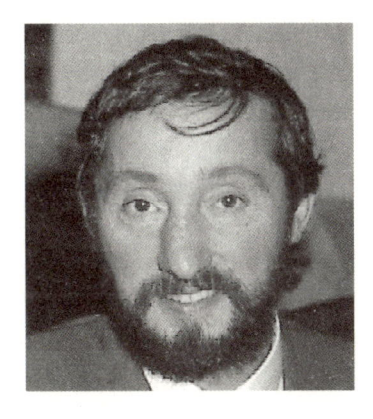

Jim Clarke

But then in the late '80s it all fell apart. Jim took out a second mortgage to invest in a scheme which promised brilliant returns. Instead, it yielded nothing — and though in the end he did receive some compensation, it was too late to save him from having to sell the farm. In due course, the Clarkes found a new home at Cashes Green, the other side of Stroud, the Slad Valley Press acquired new premises and by the mid-90s Simon and Louise had flown the nest: Simon to a job in Hongkong and Louise to a new life in Holland.

The new owners of Furners Farm were then Simon and Julie Cooper, woodcarver and gilder, and their family, who didn't have far to come, having previously lived just up the hill in Bisley. When Yvonne Dunn left for a retirement flat in Stroud, Furners Farm Cottage had been sold separately and belonged for a time to cowman Phil Manning and his wife, Anne. Some years later, when they departed, the Coopers were able to buy it back.

A new lake for Caragh

There is a golden beech tree now on the grassy island where the Furners Farm track meets the road. Beneath it is a plaque to say the tree is for Caragh Joy Cooper "from all her friends in Elcombe" and with the following lines inscribed:

> May the wind blow you joy,
> May the sun shine down joy on you,
> May your days pass with joy,
> May the night be a gift of joyful peace!
> May the dawn bring you joy in its coming.

Caragh was the daughter of Simon and Julie Cooper, to whom — along with her brothers, Daniel and Brendon —she had brought great joy in her short life. But in June 1999, just three months after her 12th birthday, that life was tragically cut short when she was run over in the street by her school near Gloucester.

For the funeral at Bisley church, Caragh's coffin was carried up the hill from Elcombe on a flower-decked cart drawn by her own pony. The burial was at Slad churchyard, where she joined earlier generations of Elcombe people to rest within line of sight of her old home.

Caragh's loss was one that her parents found very hard to bear. Before long, however, they found the consolation of a beautiful memorial. In the corner of a field below their farm, there were signs of an old millpond, which possibly fed Vatch Mill in the valley below. Though it was totally silted up and grassed over, the Coopers excavated the pond and restored it as a small lake, making a feature on the landscape that anyone looking out over the fields can enjoy.

They called it Caragh Lake — as their daughter herself had been named after another Caragh Lake in Ireland — and they were hoping that this name would be officially adopted for future Ordnance Survey maps of the valley.

Fletchers Knapp

Standing at the back of the Furners Farm yard, this was previously known as Ferners Cottage and probably started life as an outhouse or barn before becoming a tied cottage for farm workers. Under its new name it has been dramatically extended into a desirable country residence, still retaining the stables which housed Stan Fletcher's carthorses, but with its pigsties and another outbuilding now converted for human occupation.

The first tenant of the cottage (1915-20?) was possibly Donald Ayres, who had relatives at Snow's Farm further up the valley. Other early occupants, for a short period in the 1920s or '30s, were a Mr and Mrs White. Not much is known about them, except that he worked at a shop in Stroud, while she must have been unwell or unhappy or both.

Gwen Fern (Yew Tree) recalled that on one occasion Mrs White tried to cut her throat and was taken to hospital with a towel around her neck in Fletcher's car. "My mother had to sit up with her, because at the hospital they wouldn't take responsibility for suicides." Later, according to Gwen, she succeeded in taking her own life by the unusual expedient of throwing herself out of a motorcycle sidecar.

From the 1930s, the cottage was occupied by Fletcher's cowman, Frank Bartlett and his wife Elsie. Frank, who was Arthur Sam Bartlett's fifth son, worked for Fletcher for 40 years and stayed until 1970. He died five years later. His daughter, Janet, was born in 1937 and lived on the farm for the first half of her life.

Furners Farm went to auction in 1976 in two lots: the

Site of the old millpond at the bottom of Furner's field, with Under Catswood just visible on the hillside in the distance

farmhouse with eight acres and the cottage with 40 acres. The cottage and land were bought by farmer Robert Maddocks, who soon after passed on the cottage to his brother, Ian. But Ian didn't stay long and in 1980 the newly-named Fletcher's Knapp was bought by Dermot and Caroline Byrne, both veterinarians, who had just returned from seven years in New Zealand. They gave the house a major extension when they converted a large attached barn, which they purchased at the same time, to make a spacious hall and living room with bedrooms above. In 1995, the much-enlarged house was put on the market at £300,000 but not sold, and the Byrnes decided to stay.

In addition to bringing up her four children – Liam, Dominic, Sarah and Sam – Caroline was working as a Ministry of Agriculture vet and in the 1990s faced the painful job of putting down large numbers of cattle infected with BSE (Bovine Spongiform Encephalosomething). It meant an injection of 100-150ml of barbiturate (20 times the dose that would kill a human), but they were often crazed, aggressive and had to be sedated first. At the height of the crisis, Caroline was far from satisfied that the slaughterhouse measures announced by the government to protect human health were actually working. And only a few years later, she would have to cope with a mass slaughter of farm animals affected by a nationwide outbreak of foot-and-mouth disease.

Dermot Byrne reckoned the whole farm formerly belonged either to the Lypiatt or Steanbridge estates, because the standard of building work was of a quality that a small farmer wouldn't have been able to afford.

Conversion of an outbuilding at Fletcher's Knapp in the 1990s awaits installation of the septic tank

AROUND THE HOUSES

Habricia & Linden Cottages

These are the only two attached cottages in Elcombe, and since they were in the same ownership for most of the 20th century (and possibly earlier) there is a logic for treating them together.

A deed of 1827 indicates that Habricia Cottage – or both – were then owned by Sarah Tranter, the widow of Joseph Tranter, who in 1795 had bought another pair of attached cottages just next door on the site of today's Elcombe Cottage. When Joseph Tranter died, his cottages passed to his son, Joseph junior, so Sarah apparently took the house next door.

While having no further information about the Tranters, one could speculate on the possibility of their having given their name to Tranter's Hill. On the other hand, it could be mere coincidence: the name Tranter – meaning someone who makes his living with a horse and cart – is not such an uncommon one. But there is good circumstantial evidence to support another piece of Elcombe's oral history: that Habricia at some time in the past was a smithy. Digging in the adjacent garden of Yew Tree Cottage in the 1970s and '80s, one was regularly turning up horseshoes of all shapes and sizes.

Sometime late in the 19th century the property was in the hands of a Henry Morris Ash; then in 1900 it was bought by Richard Durn and his wife Elizabeth (née King), another of the numerous King clan (see Elcombe Cottage below). Richard Durn died that same year and Elizabeth in due course married Alfred White, licensee of The Star Inn in Slad. Presumably she moved to live with him, for the cottages were then rented out for a long while. After Alfred died, Elizabeth White took over and was for many years in charge at The Star. The cottages remained with the Durn family for more than 50 years, passing from Elizabeth on her death in 1937 to Arthur Durn, a wine merchant's assistant in Bournemouth, and 10 years later to Elsie Grace Darling Durn, the postmistress at Uplands and cousin of another Richard Durn (who was also related to the Bartletts of Springfield Cottage).

Some of the tenants of Habricia after 1900 included, in rough chronological order, Daniel Hitchings, Mrs Smith, Louisa Harrison, Mr and Mrs Mansell, and Mr and Mrs Nealon and their daughter Monica. According to John Myles, Louisa Harrison was there when his family arrived in the 1940s, and she was his source for the story

Elizabeth White and her second husband, Alfred, outside their pub, the Star Inn at Slad, which had been Elcombe's 'local' for generations until it was closed in 1978

of the hidden treasure of opals brought back from Australia by Will King, who she called 'Uncle Bill'. In Miss Harrison's time, there was a wooden lean-to on the end of her cottage, where Graham Wenman later built his notorious, picture-windowed studio extension in the 1960s. Of the other tenants, Mr Nealon had a motorbike and 'worked away a lot', while Mrs Nealon had been in domestic service at one of the big houses in the valley. The Mansells arrived just after WWII; he had just been demobbed and tried to start a local delivery service, though without great success. His wife was an epileptic and suffered from quite bad fits; the young John Myles was alarmed one day to find her collapsed by her front door, but then farmer's wife Lottie Fletcher arrived on her milk round and reassured him the fit would soon pass.

Among others, Linden Cottage was home to Charles King, Elsie Cox (the second Mrs Tuck) and the Hintons, who had a son and two daughters. Mr Hinton's father was (or had been) landlord at the Woolpack, so for a time Elcombe was well connected in Slad's drinking circles!

'A bit queer'

After Elsie Durn, who was also a niece of Old Will King (Elcombe Cottage), the cottages went to auction in 1952 but failed to reach the reserve price. They were bought privately for £500 the pair by Mr and Mrs Wenman, who happened to be on holiday in the area from their job running a children's home near Reading. Evelyn (Evie) Wenman was originally from Randwick, another pretty village in the Stroud hinterland, where her mother had run the post office, and she was looking to move back to the area for their retirement. With the cottages, they also inherited a sitting tenant, Mrs Carrie Wynn, who stayed on several years. A real old Gloucestershire type, she looked like a witch, smoked a pipe and had a long black trailing skirt. She walked to town once a week on Fridays to get her pension and meet her friends in a pub, then took a taxi home. She paid three shillings a week rent. Her son lived at The Vatch, and a daughter and sister nearby. At home, Graham Wenman recalled, she "sat by the fire with the dirt all around her – she was a bit queer. Her daughter came up from time to time, but they were not very good friends." This Carrie Wynn had been in domestic service in London but was by now in her 80s. It seems she was related to the other Carrie Wynn, who farmed at The Camp, and also to the Ferns of Yew Tree Cottage. In her last years she began to suffer from delusions, Gwen Wenman recalls, and would hear horses galloping past the cottage. In the end she was taken away to a nursing home.

For the first few years, the Wenmans used the cottage for holidays, sometimes bringing children from the home they were running. Then they retired and moved in permanently, visited frequently by their architect son, Graham, and his wife, Gweneth. Old Mr Wenman took a retirement job with the Post Office and, according to a neighbour, was "a big fat jolly postman with a beaming smile," always ready to give friends a lift into Stroud on his Lambretta. He died in 1965 and Evie Wenman, living on her own in Linden Cottage, survived him by 25 years. During that time, with the help of her son, she wrote a book on her early years entitled *Randwick and Roundabout*. Graham and Gwen occupied Habricia and retired there in 1983. But Graham had a close – some might say claustrophobic – relationship with his mother, to the detriment of his marriage, which ended in divorce. Gwen moved away, first to Scotland and then to a house on the outskirts of Stroud, while Graham moved into Linden Cottage with his mother and sold

Habricia to a painter from London, Peter Joseph, and his partner, Denise Ward. It was only after his mother died at an advanced age in about 1990 that Graham proposed to Gwen that they remarry. Plans for this were going ahead happily when Graham died suddenly in 1992.

As an architect, Graham Wenman was an uncompromising modernist. After qualifying, he enthusiastically joined London County Council's 'tall blocks development group', followed by 20 years as Deputy and Regional Architect with the Northwest Thames Regional Health Authority. At Elcombe, where everyone tried to build in Cotswold stone if their means permitted it, Graham was proud of his garage, his rose arch and other garden constructions made of concrete blocks.

A sloop called Squirrel

In the late '50s and early '60s, Graham made something rather more impressive than these. At the top of the Pitch, quite a long way from any open water, on his weekends and holidays he succeeded in building a 4-ton sloop. Planks for the boat were bent with steam brought into the garden by his mother. They later cracked, 'which they shouldn't have done' – but it didn't matter. When complete, he used to sail the boat regularly from Wolverstone on the east coast.

A rather shy personality, Graham had other talents besides. He amassed a considerable collection of rare books and wrote two small volumes himself entitled *Regeneration: A New Look at Indus Valley Sacred Ritual* and *Resurrection: A New Look at Early Aegean Sacred Ritual*. He had obviously read widely on both subjects and used these books to put forward some theories of his own. He also penned a series of hand-produced 'Elcombe Epics' for the children of the hamlet, including Simon and Louise Clarke, Louise Neville and Leonora and Fabian Sharp. After his death, Graham's library was sold at Sotheby's for £23,000 – the most valuable lot being a 15th century German book which fetched £3,000.

Graham's home-built sailing boat had been named Squirrel after a pet mouse of Gwen's. Now if all of her pets had turned into boats, Graham would have had a considerable naval fleet. At one point, when she had returned to Linden Cottage after his death, there were 20 bantam hens with names like Fluffy and Sweetie occupying the top room in the house, with French doors to the garden. Gwen prepared

The sloop called Squirrel takes shape on The Pitch, 650 feet above sea level. Graham Wenman (left) watches as a helper takes the strain

them gourmet meals and sang them a lullaby each evening. But then she became very ill – poisoned by the prescriptions of some Chinese herbalist quack – and fearing that she would be unable to look after them, she had all the bantams put down. In fact, though her feet remained nerve-dead, she slowly recovered and in a while was well enough to take a driving test and buy herself a car.

Before the Wenmans, Linden had been called Minden Cottage, possibly recalling the Battle of Minden (1759) during the Napoleonic wars, or perhaps more likely a soldier who got to that German town in World War I. Either way, the Wenmans decided to lay to rest the apparent military association.

Kenwood Cottage

Half-way down the Pitch, Kenwood is probably the prettiest of the cottages, but this can only be appreciated from the lawn approaching the front door, which faces the combe and Tranter's Wood and is therefore unseen by anyone but visitors to the house.

Little information is to hand on the history of the cottage or its owners and occupants before the 20th century. One piece of oral history that had reached Elcombe's oldest resident of the 1980s (Evie Wenman) was that Kenwood was once a schoolhouse, but no evidence has been found to confirm this. John Bartlett and his numerous family are thought by some to have been there at the time of the 1851 census, but because the cottages had no names at that time the census does not indicate who lived in which.

In the 1920s, Kenwood was the home of 'Grannie' Knight, a Londoner remembered by Gwen Fern (Yew Tree) as "a real lovable character". The house was dirty, but 'Grannie' welcomed visitors at any time and would always offer them a cup of tea. She had rags dipped in some special preparation to keep away foxes.

After Mrs Knight (and possibly another couple in between), the next people seem to have been Mr and Mrs Charlie Green. Mrs Green was the sister of Bill Tuck (Woodside), while all that seems to be remembered of Charlie are his regular Saturday night fights with the Bartletts after an evening at the pub. The cottage was then taken over by their son, Fred, who became better known as 'Sloppy' or 'Clergy' Green. Given that he was a milkman with farmer Phillips at Woodlands, two miles down the valley, perhaps the first nickname was acquired from milk slopping out of his churns as he made his rounds. No one has explained the second. Anyway, Fred Green's principal claim to fame is that at Easter 1922 it was he, while making his milk round, who found Florence Tuck, his aunt by marriage, drowned in Steanbridge Pond.

Fred married Iris and they had a son Alan, born around 1930. Dr John Myles (Elcombe Cottage) remembers in the 1940s playing with Alan and "a boy called John who was billeted on them". He also remembers that Alan kept ferrets in a little outbuilding just above the cottage: "These fierce little horrors were a great source of fascination to other youngsters, though none of us were brave enough to handle them."

Later, Fred Green worked as a porter on the railway. He would bicycle home for lunch – if there was any time left after drinks on the way at The Fountain (in Slad Road) or The Star. According to Graham Wenman, his son Alan made history when he rigged up the first electric light in Elcombe – battery powered – in Kenwood's outside toilet. Alan later moved to London.

For a time the Greens had a lodger from Slad, Jack Eyers, who was then in his 20s. Jack, whose grandfather had lived at Elcombe, later went on to become a well-known builder in Slad and was still living there at the turn of the millennium.

Kenwood Cottage

Iris Green told the author they had rented the cottage from a man whose father had been 'the Elcombe baker'. If he baked on the premises and supplied the local community, that must have been back in the 19th century, because early in the 20th bread was being collected from Slad.

In the 1960s, Kenwood Cottage was bought by two London ladies of the theatre, Josephine Stroud and Judith Craig. As long as they continued to work – Josephine as a theatrical agent and Judith in stage management – they spent weekends and holidays in Elcombe, moving in permanently when they retired and sold their London house around 1980. By the end of the '90s they were the third longest-standing owners after the Myles (Elcombe Cottage) and the Wenmans (Linden).

At some point, the owners of Kenwood Cottage acquired the nearly 10 acres of woodland around and up to the top of the combe, between Tranters Hill and the land of Under Catswood. For many years, Jo and Judith had as their woodsman, general handyman and supplier of logs another venerable Slad countryman, Roy Clements. Every Sunday one would see Roy's old white pickup truck trundling gently down the lane and almost find oneself thinking, 'Ah well, Roy's come – all's right with the world.'

Roy lived at Bulls Cross and had a regular job with the forestry team at the Miserden Estate a few miles away. A quiet, shy man, he nevertheless had a well-informed interest in current affairs and a keen sense of justice where he could see it was not being done. When he died in the late 1990s, many people who had known and liked him attended the funeral.

Elcombe Cottage

The old cottages on this site – a terrace of two or three – were demolished in the early 1920s and replaced with the present one-up, one-down gabled doll's house 10 years later. But this property has the oldest deeds we know of, dating from 1769, and some interesting history.

Before 1769, two cottages were owned by a joiner, Henry Viner, and later his widow, Jane, who in that year sold them to a baker, William Jennings. Although the deeds of sale then and later refer to two cottages at what was then called Elcombe Bottom, the possibility of a third in separate ownership arises from details in the 1851 census seeming to indicate three households, and from the 1769 deed which describes the property as "having a house heretofore of one Samuel R Morgan on the west side thereof." This could only otherwise refer to the now derelict cottage in the grounds of Yew Tree Cottage, believed by some to have been a bakery, but there is no known evidence as to when this was ever in use.

In any case, our worthy tradesmen, Viner and Jennings, were only landlords. Sometime earlier than 1769, the cottages were occupied by a Samuel Eagles and Richard Bousley (or Bowley), but at that time by Robert Clissold and Mary Shensall (or Sherwell). Here it gets interesting, bearing in mind that bit of oral history which says Elcombe used to have its own pub. Because the Clissold family, which had been in Bisley since the 1570s or earlier, had almost a monopoly on the local pub trade in the late 18th century. Robert Clissold, one can guess, was almost certainly in the business, and after him two younger members of the family (presumably his sons) occupied Elcombe Cottages. One was Joseph Clissold, landlord at The Bell in Bisley High Street, while the other, John, also had his occupation listed as 'innholder'. Another member of the family, Thomas, presided at the New Bear – and yet another, Samuel, was also listed as innkeeper. A census of Bisley innkeepers compiled in 1781 unfortunately doesn't make clear where John was pulling the pints, but a drinking house in Elcombe must be a possibility. Joseph Clissold died in 1794 and John in 1806.

In the meantime, the cottages had been sold to Joseph Tranter, snr., in 1795. They then passed to his son, Joseph junior, who sold them to John Dee of Eastcombe in 1834 for £49. The occupants at that time were Mary Wright, Thomas Snow and the first in a succession of Kings, who stayed for more than 110 years.

The King dynasty

Back in 1560 there had been an Edward Kinge living in Bisley, and his Will was very specific about what he would leave to his four sons. To his son William he left "a pair of tuckars cherys"; to Walter, "his best tuckars cherys and two sheep"; to Francis, "one sheep", and to Edward "his worst cherys and two sheep". Whatever they made of the tuckars cherys, the Kinge sons evidently went forth and multiplied. By 1689, the Kings were also in the nearby hamlet of Tunley, where John King also had three sons. By 1831 there were several Kings in Bisley, all owning their own houses and James alone owning five.

The first of the family to come to Elcombe was Thomas, who was a tenant of one of the Elcombe Cottages in 1827. He was followed by Charles King (son?), a shoemaker, and in 1869 by George King (grandson?), described as a labourer, who shortly afterwards bought both cottages – one owned by the Guardians of the Poor of the Stroud Union, which he got for £11.10.0. George lived to the ripe age of 86, dying in 1907 a few months before his wife, Martha Louise, aged 80. They were buried together at Holy Trinity Church in Slad, along with one of their sons, Henry, who at the age of 52 predeceased them by a couple of years. Their gravestone faces out across the valley with a direct view to Elcombe.

The cottages then passed to another son, William Davis 'Old Will' King, who must have been quite a character, though personal details about him are thin. What we know is that he went to Australia to seek his fortune prospecting for gold – and came back having done rather well for himself. He decided to pull down the old cottages and build a fine new home for himself in their place. So down they came, probably in the early 1920s, and some time later work started on the new building. The present-day cottage was the first to go up, perhaps to give Old Will somewhere to stay while the main project was completed. It has a date-stone saying '1932'. According to Gwen Fern, it was built by her uncle Walter Fern of Cockshoot, Sheepscombe, though others insist it was at least partly the work of Bill Tuck. In any event, soon afterwards things came to a standstill and the shell of Will King's new house was left unfinished. About this time Old Will lost his wits and started charging around the place threatening

AROUND THE HOUSES [119]

Taken about 1908, this is the oldest known photograph of the hamlet and shows the original Elcombe Cottages (far left)

people with an axe. He was eventually taken away by the men in white coats and died in January 1934. It was the end of Elcombe's dynasty of Kings.

Refuge from the bombs
After a short interregnum, punctuated by the start of World War II and the London Blitz, Elcombe Cottage found itself transformed into a part-time refuge for one London family anxious about the Luftwaffe's nightly raids and the safety of their children. Henry Myles was a solicitor, and his wife, May, had been born and brought up in Stroud, where her parents still lived. In November 1940, when the cottage was advertised for sale, they wasted no time catching a train from Paddington with their sons, John and David, to view the place.

...and Elcombe Cottage today

What they found, apart from a garden gone to wilderness, were the remains of Old Will King's grand design for his new house. As John Myles tells it 60 years later: "There was a roofless two-storey building with gaping windows, and this dwarfed the cottage and almost hid it. However, the cottage itself, which was only eight years old, was found to be in excellent order".

Once purchased, the cottage was furnished with a few items from Chris Wathern's junk shop at the top of Stroud High Street and others from their families. John Myles relates:

> "Galvanised buckets, essential for water-supply purposes, were bought from Smith & Lee [the former hardware store in Stroud] and are still in use sixty years on. The garden, which was a good one, was cleared and Henry Myles and Fred Green came to an arrangement whereby Fred used the garden for vegetables but the Myles's could use some of them when they were there."

Since the upper floor of Old Will's unfinished building was unstable, John and David knocked it down, but the lower storey was simply disguised by a fast-growing creeper. It was only removed in 1980, when they were building a wide new drive for their camper van.

During the war, the Myles had to travel by train and often came to Elcombe for a week or more at a time. Their bath was a canvas one, shielded from the public gaze by a groundsheet suspended along the front of the porch, and the water was heated in kettles on a tiny kitchen range. When petrol became available again after the war, the family's old black Morris saloon was taken out of storage and became a familiar sight in the hamlet.

In due course John Myles qualified as a doctor and he remembers working as an orthopaedic registrar at Paddington General Hospital in the 1960s when Dr Hugh Francis (Yew Tree Cottage) was a consultant radiologist there. More recently, John and his family have used the cottage as an occasional weekend retreat, coming from their home in Peterborough, where he has had his medical practice.

Electricity and mains water have never been connected at Elcombe Cottage, so for the Myles family the village spring, a coal fire and candles have remained essentials.

AROUND THE HOUSES

Springfield Cottage

No one today knows the site of the original grange that was 14th century Elcombe, but assuming that the lane already had to exist as a track of some sort – at least upwards in the direction of Bisley – Springfield and Woodside Cottages are perhaps the most likely. One former owner, Ron Lanchbury, claimed that Springfield dated back to 1650, though it's not known what if any evidence he had for this. The present building evidently began life as two cottages, built separately on different levels, which accounts for the irregular floor levels of the interior. One of them had its front door directly on to The Pitch, where the stone doorway is still visible in the wall.

The first owners we know of were the Bartletts (see Chapter 5). When they finally left in 1943, the cottage was bought by Miss Ibferson, who shared it with a Miss Mees, both of them working at Cheltenham College. Miss Mees then got married and moved away. Miss Ibferson was a matron, who later went into private nursing. Of Danish nationality, she was probably the first foreign resident – though by then several people in the hamlet had been abroad.

After Miss Ibferson, the cottage was bought (1974) by Ron Lanchbury, a musician who had played for some big bands in earlier years and was often still away on gigs with his group. After schooling in Cheltenham, Ron had become an apprentice piano tuner and repairer and played percussion in a local band. Five years later he went to London with his new wife, a Birdlip girl, and found work as a drummer. During WWII in the RAF, he toured Britain in a five-piece band to keep up the soldiers' morale. After the war, he played with the then-famous bands of Edmundo Ros, Joe Loss and also Sidney Lipton, with whom he stayed 17 years. In 1974, on moving to Elcombe, Ron set up his own group, The County Players, in

'Goatman' (Ron Lanchbury) with Whiz and his dog Penny

GRAHAM WENMAN

which he played the electric piano. They had a regular Saturday night gig at the Gloucestershire Sports Stadium.

In Graham Wenman's 'Elcombe Epics', Ron was known as 'Goatman', being the owner of a goat called Whiz, who for most of the time occupied the triangle of land he owned beyond the western boundary of Yew Tree Cottage. The Yew Tree deeds indicate that in 1869 this triangle was owned by Samuel Webb and previously by William Fletcher. It was attached to Springfield in Sam Bartlett's time, when his granddaughter Janet says it was a big vegetable garden, so Webb and Fletcher could have been previous owners of this cottage.

In 1980, under the title 'UFOs in Elcombe?', the second issue of the Slad Valley News reported: "There was great excitement in the Lanchbury household in Elcombe when at 12.40am one night at the end of March, Mr Ron Lanchbury saw a glow of orange lights about five miles away in the direction of Selsley Common." Shortly afterwards, The Times had a story about 'bright lights over Britain', but the Ministry of Defence poured cold water on the UFO theory, saying the lights were due to showers of meteorites burning up in the atmosphere. A likely story!

By then, Ron had taken a regular job at the Stroud music shop, and eventually, after his wife had a serious illness, they sold and moved to Slad in 1981. After the Lanchburys, the cottage was bought by Yvonne Dunn, a redoubtable Yorkshire lady universally known as 'Grandma', who in her widowhood wanted to be near her daughter Barbara Clarke and grandchildren Simon and Louise at Furners. In fact, after three or four years, she went one better and moved into Furners Farm Cottage, which the Clarkes had converted from a scruffy outbuilding, initially for some bed-and-breakfast income.

Next came the Hoopers, a weekender couple with a computer business in the Reading area, but they didn't stay long before selling to Richard Morris, a senior teacher at Beaudesert Park preparatory school, Minchinhampton, where one of his pupils had been Fabian of Yew Tree Cottage. Richard's daughter, Jessica, stayed with him while taking a course at Cirencester College and then moved to London. His son, Andrew, was a traveller who was often camped somewhere in the area and visited from time to time.

Towards the end of the '90s, Richard thought it was time to move and put his house on the market. But then, like the Byrnes at Fletchers Knapp, he changed his mind and decided to stay. Once under Elcombe's spell, it seems, farewell is the hardest thing to say.

AROUND THE HOUSES

Woodside

Approaching Elcombe from Swift's Hill, Woodside Cottage is the first house one comes to. Aptly named, it is tucked into the lee of Tranter's Hill Wood right at the bottom of the combe, set back from the road by the width of the small grassy bank in front of it which gives access to the Elcombe spring.

The first owner that people can remember was 'Butcher Pole' or William Pole to give him his proper name, who was there around 1915 but possibly earlier. He had five children and his own butcher's shop near the Cross in Stroud.

Bill Tuck must have been there by 1920, because it was only a year or two later that his first wife, Florence, drowned herself in Steanbridge pond (see Chapter 6). And he stayed for half a century. As John Papworth records in his Rural Notebook:

Woodside Cottage

"The end came when Stanley the cowman [Stanley Burton, who worked for the Fletchers] at the neighbouring farm took his milk in as usual one morning and found the old man was unable to get up from his bed. He was taken to a local institution for old people but at the end of the winter he said he felt better, which he was, and that he wanted to return. But reason, logic, convenience, hygiene, progress and civilisation, to say nothing of cash and the lack of an extended network of family relationships which in less besotted times helped to guard us at both ends of life – and in the middle too if need be – were against him. Then a new complication arose: how did he suppose the bills for his keep in the institution were paid? He wasn't a pauper was he? Didn't he have some property? Well then... So now, while he lingers on, his beloved cottage and garden are put up for sale and strangers poke and sniff and haggle..."

The cottage was sold to a Miss Hogg, a teacher at Cheltenham College and friend of Miss Ibferson next door. One story says that she never really wanted the place because she had her own flat in Cheltenham, and she seems to have used it only for weekends. But she didn't stay very long and the cottage was then acquired by a London-based businessman, Michael Court, for whom it has also been a weekend retreat.

Michael Court became renowned for his succession of smart Porsche cars, but most of the time he declined invitations to Elcombe social gatherings and kept himself to himself, as the saying goes. Until, that is, he prompted the 1990s Drama of the Decade by erecting gates and a fence around the bank to the spring. That story is recounted in the next chapter.

The mystery cottage

Belonging to a friend of Richard Morris (Springfield), this 19th century painting by Charles H. Sansom is entitled 'View at Elcombe, Near Stroud, Glos'. But neither the cottage nor its surroundings resembles anything in the hamlet today. There is another tiny place called Elcombe, nearer to Dursley than Stroud, but Richard has been there to check and found nothing like the picture. The recollection of a visit, one has to guess, with more artistic licence than actuality

11   PROPERTY AT ISSUE
     Not in my back yard!

Property is theft, said Proudhon. But as long as private property is legal, the English are going to squabble over it, and in this respect Elcombe is simply a microcosm of the country at large. In earlier times, one can imagine that people here came to blows over food, money, politics, personal insults or love affairs. In the late 20th century, largely insulated from the vagaries of their neighbours' personal or business lives, the thing that got people most agitated was other people messing about with their houses or land.

In 1966, the Slad Valley was designated an Area of Outstanding Natural Beauty (AONB) – justly in the eyes of the many Gloucestershire folk who regard it as the most beautiful and unspoilt of the valleys along the Cotswold escarpment. This should mean that Stroud District planners, unless overruled by the Department of the Environment, will not allow a McDonalds or a Coca Cola factory to be built in the middle of it. What it should mean in terms of rights and restrictions for the people who actually live here is much more a bone of contention. And regardless of the AONB, there is a serious question as to whether a property developer or private homeowner should be able to override the concerted opposition of a village's residents to put up a building that they consider an ugly or unwanted intrusion.

While the valley's nine farmhouses, including Furners, were all reasonably spacious family residences, the cottages were almost uniformly minuscule: one living room, one or at most two bedrooms and a kitchen for a family often of seven, eight or more. So while the farms have not needed much enlargement for modern, smaller families, the cottages have absorbed a large amount of their owners' rising incomes. And if they have hardly increased in number during the 20th century they must have expanded 50 per cent or more in the

[125]

volume of living accommodation. Those that have been substantially added to or remodelled in this period include Rose Cottage, Hillside, Yew Tree, Habricia, Linden, Fletcher's Knapp, Kenwood and Woodside. That only leaves Under Catswood, which wasn't built until half way through the century but has been significantly extended since, and Springfield and Elcombe Cottages, which have changed little or not at all.

Extensions and dissensions

While he was at Habricia Cottage, Graham Wenman added a section on the end of it with a large, timber-framed picture window. What objections his scheme aroused at the time are not now known, but it has prompted plenty of hostile comments since. In 1994, the Daily Mail ran an article about botched home extensions and singled out Habricia Cottage for special mention and a photo, saying that anyone meandering through the picturesque valley would be "visually assaulted by a glass-and-concrete structure on the side of a mellow stone cottage". Graham later made an extension at the other end of Linden Cottage, but this time clad in traditional stone, as the Council by then would have insisted; and he followed this with another one climbing up the garden at the back.

In the mid-1980s, Yew Tree Cottage also underwent a major enlargement, but this was achieved (of necessity) without increasing its 'footprint' on the ground. By what was essentially a loft conversion and the incorporation of lean-tos behind the house to form an internal landing, the Sharps gained two bedrooms and a bathroom on the new top floor and an extra bedroom – previously the landing – on the middle floor. The cottage when first built (18thC?) had two rooms, one above the other, joined by a steep coracle stone staircase. At the back of the living room-cum-kitchen was a deep larder hewn into the rock against which it was set.

Habricia Cottage was one of several houses photographed to illustrate this Daily Mail article.

PROPERTY AT ISSUE

Soon after, another two rooms were added on the west side. Then there was a lengthy interval until the 1930s, when two more rooms were added on the east side – a washhouse (now the kitchen) and a bedroom above. A proper bathroom had to wait until the 1960s.

Most of Elcombe's cottages began the same way, being built with stone from the Swift's Hill quarry. In the last few years, one new dwelling has been added to the hamlet's housing stock with the conversion by Dermot Byrne of pigsties and other outbuildings at Fletcher's Knapp to make a single-storey cottage.

During the 1980s, various of his neighbours entered objections to Graham's planning applications. But, claiming that they were needed by his aged mother, he managed to get them passed.

Artistic licence

The next saga came in 1988, when Stroud planners, after concerted objections from Elcombe, turned down an application by painter Peter Joseph and his partner Denise Ward to build a studio at the top of their garden. Soon afterwards, Denise Ward wrote to a neighbour: "We have found ourselves devestated not only by the knowledge that extensive practical difficulties may now have been made permanent by this decision; but also by knowing that there are people who uninhibitedly use the supposedly unarguable morality of 'conservation' attached to ideas based on middle-class sentimentality to put a sledge hammer through our hopes." The Josephs won their appeal to the Department of the Environment and, at the cost of much ill-feeling on all sides, the studio was built.

Behind Habricia and Linden Cottages, the contentious late 20th century sprawl, which someone likened to a Brazilian *favela*: Peter Joseph's studio (left) and two Wenman add-ons. The taller of the latter has since been demolished

Enclosing the commons

Not very long afterwards, however, the studio saga was eclipsed by an even bigger row over ownership and use of the grassy bank around the spring. (Everyone calls it 'the spring', which sounds nicer, but strictly speaking it is a spout, as most maps attest, since rather than

ALL ABOUT ELCOMBE

Peter Joseph's studio was not without its defenders, including the 89-year-old architectural luminary Berthold Lubetkin, who, however, slightly spoiled things by entering a Nimby protest of his own against the conversion of his former home in another Gloucestershire hamlet

rising naturally the water is piped down from the fields at the top of the combe.) This row was provoked when Michael Court, owner of the adjacent Woodside Cottage, put up a post-and-chain fence along the road in front of the bank and gates to the gravel drive leading to his garage. A number of meetings were held by an ad hoc residents' committee which felt strongly that Mr Court had no right to enclose what had always been a public piece of land. For his part, Michael Court insisted he was within his rights and that the fence was to discourage outsiders from picnicking outside his window, which he claimed they were doing more and more.

"Throughout last summer," he declared, "on every weekend I was at my cottage I had problems with people who amongst other things parked on the grass verge, parked in my drive, had picnics on the grass with screaming children running riot and their dogs defecating on the grass".   Negotiations failed and the committee assembled affidavits from many past and present residents to prove there was an established right of way to the spring. In the meantime, some less patient objectors chopped down the fence posts, which Michael Court promptly replaced in metal, though this time with a gap for access. One evening, while these posts were being installed, an angry Gerry Vaughan, one of the regular users of the spring, attacked them with an axe and had to be restrained by force. This was the Saturday Night Crisis of February '96. There was much shouting and recrimination and the police were called.

Six months later, Michael Court's gates were removed by a person or

PROPERTY AT ISSUE

persons unknown. After the first fence was destroyed, he had installed a security camera (though some said it was a dummy) and he offered to remove this if his gates were returned. They weren't, but one of them was found some time later covered in leaves on Tranters Hill. In the meantime, a public right of way had been formally approved. It was left to the Council's Highways Dept to pursue removal of the fence and gates, which Mr Court was continuing to dispute. One of the leading objectors claimed that even if villagers didn't meet around the spring any more, it had a greater – even universal – symbolic

WWWELCOME TO ELCOMBE

To find out what 'Elcombe' might mean to the wider world, the simple method nowadays is to ask one's favourite search engine. Google, for example, turns up 2,000 web pages with references to the name.

There's a property firm somewhere called Elcombe Estates, a high-tech company in Canada called Elcombe Systems Ltd, while the Elcombe in the Isle of Wight is a bed-and-breakfast with "splendid views". There's also a page about an Australian fiddler called Charlie Batchelor, who used to play in Elcombe, New South Wales.

But the great majority of entries on the world-wide web are of people with the family name of Elcombe. And, from a scan of the first hundred on the listing, most would appear to be resident in the United States and Canada, with fewer in the UK and Australia. (At the time of writing there are no Elcombes in the Gloucestershire or London telephone directories.)

So perhaps our founding father, Edmund de Elcomb, Perpetual Vicar of Bisley, has succeeded in perpetuating his line across the centuries and around the globe. And - who knows? - maybe Claire Elcombe of Arizona, who is researching her family tree, will eventually be able to trace her ancestors back to him.

significance: "We don't meet around the spring any more to exchange news, but perhaps we can maintain – in the continuing use of this spring area – a symbolic recognition that as a community we share a dependency on resources that are essential to life, and that to forget this endangers our social fabric as well as our planet." About the same time a bacteriological examination of the spring water had shown some contamination, leading to an 'Unfit to Drink' sign being installed by the Health Authority. The water later tested clear and the sign was removed.

In the course of this dispute, Denise Ward wrote to Mr Sutton, Michael Court's builder and friend, who had allegedly met Gerry at the spring and told him he would hold him personally responsible for any further attempt to remove the gates or fence. According to Ward, the implication of Sutton's warning was clearly a threat of physical violence. She retaliated with an implied threat of her own to Mr Sutton and/or his business, prompting a warning letter from Court's solicitors. In his own reply, Mr Sutton offered a somewhat different version but stressed that he had had no intention of threatening anyone, despite Gerry's alarming appearance and gestures:

> "When Gerard Vaughan was hacking at Mr Court's fence he was hooded and made a very frightening figure so late at night. He would not stop when asked and indeed it was Mr Court who called the police when Mr Vaughan held the axe above my head. It was then I was very frightened and tried to reason with him. I said anything that came to mind just to make him put the axe down. I am not a violent man and your inference that I might resent Mr Vaughan because of his unconventional life style is very wrong. In a way I envy his life style and genuinely wish him to be left alone."

Later, those involved succeeded in establishing that ownership of the spring bank had never left the County Council's Highways Department. Highways gave Mr Court an ultimatum for removing the fence, and though he appealed it was eventually replaced with the County Council's standard issue posts. His gates were allowed to remain. As one resident commented wryly, the new official posts were "probably uglier than what was there before". Others consoled themselves with the fact that an important issue of principle had been defended. The lesson seems to be, unfortunately, that truth is not always beauty, nor beauty truth!

Was Proudhon right?
Perhaps there is a little niggling voice in all of us, asking if Proudhon could have been right. Certain it is, surely, that every new house extension and every new garage is stealing a little something from anyone who had a right to expect this valley to be an unspoiled area of natural beauty. Certain, too, that people's desire to maximise the 'investment' in their homes has not run its course. It must be said that much remodelling of homes in Elcombe over the past 30 years

has been undertaken without any objections from neighbours. All the same, it is likely that property issues of this kind will be a potential source of conflict in the hamlet for some time to come.

THE SOUND OF SILENCE

One of the most precious qualities of Elcombe is the quality of its silence. It is never a blank silence, having a hundred different auditory colours. In the early morning, on a hazy summer afternoon, at night when traffic on the valley road has ceased, or in that special velvety quiet when everything is under snow – standing on any of the cottage terraces one can experience a perfect peace and stillness embracing the landscape and the sky. In a garden bounded by trees or other buildings it could never be the same, but here, with the whole panorama of the valley spread out below and seeming to stretch to infinity, this silence can induce a state of being – an inner tranquillity – that is hard to find in our noisy modern world.

In a sense, all the noises of Elcombe are framed by this silence. Though the combe acts as a soundbox, magnifying human voices and the sounds of animals even from a considerable distance, when they die away it is the underlying silence that will delight any sensitive ear. We hear the clock of Slad church striking the hour, the baa-ing, the neighing and the moo-ing of farm animals from fields roundabout, the shouts and laughter of families or children playing on Swifts Hill, the clip-clop of riders on the lane, the song of a blackbird sitting atop an ash tree, the squawk of a pheasant, the raucous cries of magpies and crows and, until recently, the strident call of peacocks from a farm across the valley. There'll be fragments of conversation from little knots of people with rucksacks passing by on the annual Five Valleys Walk, or the not-quite audible commentary of a guide escorting groups of 'Cider with Rosie' tourists from Slad. For many years we got to recognise the uncertain chug-chug of Gerry's motorbike and the sounds of people from further afield stopping at the spring for water. At night, all these give way to the sound of badgers rustling in the undergrowth, the wind in the trees of Tranters Hill, the occasional plaintive bark of a fox and the echoing hoots of owls around the combe. In the 1980s and early '90s, in more than one of the houses – but not outdoors – one could also hear at night a mysterious, low-pitched humming noise. At Yew Tree Cottage, it seemed to have a subterranean source, as if from the machinery of some deep underground installation, while others thought it could be transmissions from an earth satellite – but it was never explained.

During the day, there are the ever more frequent mechanical noises: the rumble of tractors, harvesters and other farm machinery, the drone of cars on the lane, the throb of an occasional helicopter, and, on summer evenings, the hot air balloons drifting across, announcing themselves with the whoosh of their burners. Unfortunately, when it comes to tending our bit of garden or countryside, the scythe and sickle are now only relics of a bygone era; in Elcombe, as elsewhere, almost everyone seems to have an expensive, screeching strimmer. In 1997, this prompted Pat Cooper in the Slad Valley News to inveigh against the noise pollution that people are inflicting on each other. "I dread the summer now," she wrote. "If it's not strimmers buzzing all day it's motor mowers or hedgetrimmers; the idea of being able to sit out on a summer's day in one's garden to enjoy the bird song, soak up the flowers' wafting perfumes and gently hear the bees buzzing is a very rare occurence now, as the infernal mechanised gardeners are 'at it' all day."

On Saturdays and Sundays, particularly, motor noise can be a blight (which might make the case for a weekend moratorium), but generally speaking for the rest of the time Elcombe is a haven of tranquillity, where one can still enjoy the sound of silence.

A cottage interior, late 20th century

12 THE FUTURE
A little fantasy

We can just about imagine what life must have been like for our forerunners in Elcombe 200 years ago. But no one of that time could have begun to guess what life would be like for us today. Electricity? – What's that? Television? – Impossible! Cars? – You must be joking!

So your imagination will have to run pretty wild to come anywhere near what Elcombe can expect a couple of centuries into the future. If you live that long, here's an advertisement – oh yes, they'll surely still have those – that you might expect to find in the SVNO (Slad Valley News Online) of April 2202:

[133]

FOR SALE

Manor house in Elcombe
Fabulous sea views – Helipad
3 guest cottages

A superb country retreat with all conceivable amenities, Old Elcombe Manor dates back at least 120 years and is constructed of traditional Cotswold titanium and reinforced perspex, with security installations designed to withstand anything from burglars to terrorist attacks. Built on the site of an ancient stone hovel destroyed in World War III, the Manor boasts unequalled panoramic views over the New Sea, which has now immersed the former town of Stroud, providing for an elegant marina at the nearby community of Vache, where the Manor has three reserved moorings.

Old Elcombe Manor has seven bedrooms, all with private terraces and en suite swimmingrooms, in the main house, and six more in the guest annexes, Lyndon, Habricia and Springwood, each accessed by high-speed tunnels. The spectacular day room (18 x 10 x 9 metres) has floor-to-ceiling multivision, a lift to the double-bay helipad and virtual windows affording panoramic views of the valley with its trees, hedges and cows as they were 250 years ago. The kitchen has a 'Magic' food system linked to 10 restaurants in the area for instant meal delivery.

The manor is protected by a 4-metre high electrified fence and an elite, 24-hour security corps from Sladlads Inc. Within two minutes of the property by gyrojet is the fashionable Summer Street esplanade, where approved, card-carrying residents can stroll around the shops, cafés and boat-hire establishments, admiring the view of yachts and small craft plying across the sound, or exploring the many private clubs offering non-stop shows of pole-dancing, lap-dancing and saunas for all tastes...

Price on application

Note to prospective purchasers: The IPCC (International Panel on Climate Change) has issued a report containing categorical assurances that the dramatic rises in sea level of the past 100 years are now at an end. Insurance is once again available on properties at least 50 metres above the high water mark.

THE FUTURE

One could pursue this manic vision, but if it doesn't get quite so bad, perhaps it'll be because there's either no more petrol, no more cars, no more helicopters (to get the billionaires here)...or no more people. By 2010 already, cars may have to be running on electric, solar or hydrogen power, which probably only the wealthiest in Elcombe will be able to afford (returning us to the 1930s). Taking an alternative prospect for 2202, one can imagine that the toll of modern plagues such as vCJD, vHIV (the devastating variant of HIV yet to be discovered), combined with ozone depletion and the non-availability of health care or other basic services outside the big cities, will have left Elcombe an abandoned backwater (returning us to the Middle Ages). A few centuries after that, perhaps there will be left only one grange, with its solitary occupant being a priest called Edmund. And in another 100 million years why not envisage the whole Cotswold escarpment once more beneath the sea whence it came?

However silly such fantasies may seem, it would be infinitely more far-fetched to think Elcombe will stay as it is. So there are grounds for supposing that perhaps the century or two on either side of the year 2000 could represent the apogee of social development for a hamlet like this. It is a sobering thought, which should cause those of us who have known it in our present lifetimes to give thanks for this enchanting place.

* * *

Sources and Further Reading

Atkins, Sir Robert, *The Ancient and Present State of Gloucestershire*, London, 1712.
Beard, Howard (Ed), *Painswick, Sheepscombe, Slad and Edge*,
    Photographic collection, Chalford Publishing, 1997.
Bisley Parish Records, Gloucester Record Office
Blair, Peter Hunter, *Anglo-Saxon England*, Folio Society, London, 1997.
Bolton, J L, *The Medieval English Economy 1150-1500*, Dent, 1980.
Darvill, Timothy, *Prehistoric Gloucestershire*, Alan Sutton, 1987.
Davis, Mollie, *The History of Winson, A Cotswold Village*, Alan Sutton, Stroud, 1992.
Fern, Jim, *Ferns in the Valley*, Millvale Ltd, 1994.
Finberg, H P R, *Gloucestershire: The History of the Landscape*, Hodder
        & Stoughton, London, 1955.
_____ (Ed), *Gloucestershire Studies*, Leicester University Press, 1957.
Fisher, Paul Hawkins, *Notes and Recollections of Stroud*, 1891,
    reprinted by Alan Sutton, Dursley, 1975.
Gloucestershire County Records
Heighway, Carolyn, *Anglosaxon Gloucestershire*, Alan Sutton, 1987.
Hill, Susan, *The Spirit of the Cotswolds*, Michael Joseph, London, 1988.
Lee, Laurie, *Cider with Rosie*, Hogarth Press, 1959.
Marshall, *The Rural Economy of Glocestershire*, Vol. 2, London, 1796.
Merrett, Wilfred (Ed), *Pubs of the Old Stroud Brewery*, Chalford Publishing, Stroud, 1996.
Papworth, John, Rural Notebook in "Resurgence," Vol 2, No 8/9, July-
        October 1969.
Rudd, Mary, *Historical Records of Bisley-with-Lypiatt*, 1937.
Shipman, Juliet, *Bisley: A Cotswold Village Remembered*, Chantry Press, Eastcombe, 1991.
Slad Valley News, 1980-1997.
Smith, A H (Ed), *Place-names of Gloucestershire, Part I*, English
    Place-name Society, Vol. 38, 1960-61, Cambridge University Press, 1964.
Tawney, R H, *The Radical Tradition*, George Allen & Unwin, 1964.
Tawney, Jeannette, Letters to her brother William (later Lord)
    Beveridge, 1933–1953, London School of Economics Archive.
Terrill, Ross, *R H Tawney and His Times: Socialism as Fellowship*,
        André Deutsch, London, 1974.
Wenman, Graham, *A New Look at Early Aegean Sacred Ritual*, Stroud Publishing, 1991.
_____ , *A New Look at Indus Valley Sacred Ritual*, Stroud
            Publishing, 1992.
_____ , "Elcombe Epics" 1-6, 1978-1982.

Interviews with the author (on audio cassette):
  Gwen Fern & Dorothy Wynn, 1983
  Evie Wenman, 1983
  Graham Wenman, 1983
  Iris Green, 1983
  Janet Bartlett, 1995
  John Papworth, 1995
  Mervyn Dickenson, 1997.

Index

By Subject

Agriculture, 4, 5, 17, 19
Anglo-Saxons, 8
BSE, 108
Buried treasure, 41
Caragh Lake, 106
Celts, 4-5, 9
Census of 1851, 18, 82
Chalford Brass Band, 31
Children, 34
Christianity, 8
Cider with Rosie 40, 52, 101, 104, 131
Climate, 2, 34
Cotswold snails, 7
Crime and violence, 21
Dialect, 49
Dobunni, 5
Domesday Book, 9
Elcombe Epics, 7, 48, 112, 122
Electricity, 25, 27, 69, 120
Fabian Society, 56
Ferrets, 45, 48
Flora & fauna, 29, 39
Food, 26, 37
Fuel, 26, 29
Gardens, 26, 33, 50
Ghost, 37
Gloucestershire Wildlife Trust, 40
Glowworms, 1, 27
Gypsies, 40
Highways Dept, 129
Holidays, 32
House extensions, 125-6
Hwicce, 8
London School of Economics, 55-6, 58, 61
Long barrows, 3
Mills, 13, 15, 17, 36, 43
Mortimer estates, 11, 13
Neolithic bones, 6
Neolithic period, 3
Noise pollution, 132

Normans, 9
Norse, 9
Occupations, 19, 24
Oolitic limestone, 2
Peace News, 75
Pets, 48, 112
Population, 9, 13, 19
Postal service, 23
Property values, 20, 24-5, 108
Romans, 5-8
Shops, 20, 50
Silence, 131
Slad Society, 105
Slad Valley Press, 105
Slad Valley News, 32, 122, 132
Sounds, 131
Stroud News (and Journal), 23, 68
Spies, 67, 76
Telephones, 66
Titanic, 103
Townsends Flour Mill, 45
Transport, 23, 28, 70, 102
Vikings, 9
Water, 25, 28, 66-7, 120
Weather, 66, 69
Windmill, 78, 99
Woodland clearances, 5
Wool trade, 19
Workers' Educational Association, 55-6, 59
World War I, 31, 49-50, 56-7, 95
World War II, 25-6, 47, 58, 61, 67-8, 119, 121
www.elcombe, 129

By People

Alfred, King, 9
Adams, Charles and Margaret, 84
Alcock, Guy, 104
Alexander of Duntisbourne, 12
Archbishop of Canterbury, 56

[138]

INDEX

Arndell, Thomas, 100
Ash, Henry Morris, 109
Attlee, Clement, 56
Ayres, Donald, 107
Bailey, Rosie, 89
Bartelet, Iohannes, 45
Bartlett, Arthur Sam, 45, 121
Bartlett, Frank & Elsie, 46, 107
Bartlett, Janet, 45-8, 84, 101
Bartlett, John and family, 18, 45-47, 86, 100, 114
Bartlett, Reg, 21, 46
Beveridge, William (Lord), 56, 61-7
Bishop, Walter, 82, 95
Blake, George, 76
Bodenham family, 47, 93-4
Bousley, Richard, 117
Brown, Arthur & Gertrude, 86
Brown, Jack, 31
Brown, Leslie, 54, 86-7
Buck, Pearl, 71
Buckingham, Marquis of, 13
Byrne, Dermot & Caroline, 108, 127
Carey, Michael & Diana, 85
Castro, Fidel, 75
Ceawlin, 8
Charles I, King, 1, 13
Clarke, Jim & Barbara, 104-5, 122
Clavill, Richard de, 12
Clements, Roy, 115-6
Clissold family, 117
Clissold, Joseph & John, 20
Clissold, Thomas, 36
Close, Cecil, 53
Cobbett, William, 5
Cooper, Brian, 76-7
Cooper, Caragh, 106
Cooper, Pat, 30, 132
Cooper, Simon & Julie, 84, 105-6
Court, Michael, 124, 128
Craig, Judith, 32, 115
Critchley, Elsie, 46
Davies, Eli & Comfort, 19
Dee, John, 117
Dirty Doris, 37
Dobunni, 5, 7
Dorrington, John Edward, 17-19, 86
Dunn, Yvonne, 105, 122
Durn, Elsie, 47, 109
Durn, Richard & Eliabeth, 47, 109
Eagles, Samuel, 117

Edward II, King, 11
Elcomb, Edmund de, 11-12, 129
Enthoven, Dorothea, 87
Eyers, George, 86
Eyers, Jack, 86, 115
Fern, Arthur & family, 91-3
Fern, Gwen, 1-2, 26-7, 91-2, 118
Fitzwilliam, Jessica, 71
Fletcher, Stan & Lottie, 46-7, 70, 82, 101-4
Fletcher, William, 46
Fouquet, Marcelle, 75
Francis, Hugh & Marian, 32, 95-7, 120
Frink, Elisabeth, 97
Green, Charlie & Mrs, 46, 114
Green, Fred 'Sloppy' & family, 46, 52, 114-5
Gregory, Rachel, 20, 91, 97, 100
Haile Selassie, Emperor, 43
Hancocks, William, 21
Hanks, Lou, 37
Harrison, Louisa, 41, 63, 109-110
Harrison, Mr, 63
Harrison, Mrs, 63
Henry IV, King, 12
Henry V, King, 12
Hewison, Mr, 87
Hewitt family, 94
Heywood, (Sir) Oliver & Denise, 84-5, 99
Hirsch, Fred, 25
Hitchings family, 103
Hitchings, Daniel, 109
Hitchings, Isaac, 91
Hogg, Miss, 124
Hooper, Mr & Mrs, 122
Howarth, Sidney & Lilian, 88
Ibferson, Miss, 121
Isabella, Queen, 11
James I, King, 13
Jennings, William, 117
Jewson, Norman, 63, 87
Jones, Albert, 91
Joseph, Peter, 112, 127-8
Kaunda, Kenneth, 74-6
King(e) family, 118-9
King, George & Lucy, 19
King, Thomas & Hannah, 19
King, Will, 21, 41, 82, 110
Kohr, Leopold, 73, 78, 90
Lacey, Peter de, 12
Lanchbury, Ron, 15, 121-2

INDEX

Lee, Laurie, 40, 49-50, 52
Lewis, Thomas, 18
Lodge, Diana, 73, 79, 90
MacDonald, Ramsay, 59
Maddocks, Robert & Ian, 108
Manning, Phil & Anne, 105
Mansell, Mr & Mrs, 109
Mansell, William, 12
Mayo, Sarah, 19, 100
Mees, Miss, 121
Miles, William, 83
Morgan, Samuel R, 117
Morris, Richard, 122, 124
Mortimer, Roger de, 10
Mortimer, Roger, 11
Mutton, Mary, 45
Myles, Dr John, 110, 115, 119-20
Myles, Henry & family, 97, 119-20
Nealon, Mr & Mrs, 109-10
Neville, Nick & Ann, 85, 88, 98
Papworth, Revd John, 17, 21, 37, 49-51, 53, 60, 68, 73-80, 81, 84, 87, 90, 98, 123
Parker-Harrison, Walter, 93
Partridge, Thomas and George, 45, 101
Pegler, Mary Eliza, 86
Perkins, Clare, 87
Pole, William, 87, 123
Poulson, William, 100
Power Eileen, 56
Proudhon, Pierre-Joseph, 125
Richard, Duke of York, 13
Roffe, Victor & Jane, 48, 90
Romulus, 6
Russell, George, 91
Selwyn, Daniel & Sophia, 19, 91
Sered, William, 11
Sharp, Robin & family, 97
Sharp, Leonora & Fabian, 8, 48
Shensall, Mary, 117
Shillito, Peter & Joan, 90
Sims, William, 86
Skinner, William, 86
Snow, Thomas & Hannah, 19, 91, 118
Spicer, Sam, 86
Stanton, Anis, 11
Stanton, Arthur, 23
Stephens, Thomas, 13
Stratford, Jimmy & family, 87
Stroud, Josephine, 32, 115
Sutton, Mr, 130
Tawney, Jeanette, 6, 37, 55-6, 61-71

Tawney, R.H., 15-16, 25, 37, 55-60, 61-71, 73, 83-4, 102
Throckmorton, Francis, 15
Tranter, Joseph & Sarah, 91, 109, 117
Tuck, William & family, 49-54, 86, 118, 123
Tuck, Caleb, 53, 89
Twinning, Hubert & Jack, 37
Twinning, Wilson, 92
Tyler, Rachel, 86
Tyrell, James, 19
Vaughan, Gerry, 21, 79, 98-9, 128
Vespasian, Consul Flavius, 7
Viner, Jane, 13
Ward, Denise, 112, 127, 130
Ware, Sir Fabian, 62
Webb, Boney, 39
Webb, Samuel, 46
Wenman, Evie, 54, 111
Wenman, Graham & Gwen, 7, 21, 41, 48, 50, 83, 111-3, 126-7
White, Alfred & Elizabeth, 47, 109
White, Mr & Mrs, 107
Whiting, John, 86
Whiting, Thomas, 20, 91
Whittington, Richard (Dick), 12
Whiz, 48, 122
William, Duke of Normandy, 9
Williams, Pat, 71
Wright, Mary, 91, 118
Wynn, Carrie (Linden Cott.), 111
Wynn, Carrie (The Camp), 93, 111
Wynn, Dorothy, 91, 93

By Places

Abbey Farm, 16
Alehouse, 20, 117
Amberley, 71
Ansteads Farm, 42
Bath, 17
Bear of Bisley, The, 20, 34
Birdlip, 9
Bisley, 3, 4, 9-13, 16, 19-20, 21, 23, 32, 41, 87
  Calico Bequest, 28
  Church, 11, 106
  Common, 19
  Estate, 23
  Hundred, 10, 42

INDEX

Lock-up, 21
Manor, 12
Brothel, 20
Bulls Cross, 42
Bussage, 12
Catswood Farm, 43, 100
Cheltenham, 17, 65
Cotswolds, 3, 4, 9, 19, 35, 57
Country Elephant, The, 33
Custom Scrubs, 6, 20
Dunkite Hill Wood, 17, 19, 78, 89
Dyrham, 8
Elcombe Cottage(s), 19, 42, 82, 117-20, 126
Elcombe spring, 28, 123, 128-30
Elliott Nature Reserve, 30, 39
Fletcher's Knapp, 18, 42, 46, 90, 107-8, 127
Fosse Way, 5
Furners Farm Cottage, 18, 105, 122
Furners Farm, 15, 42, 45, 74, 76, 81, 100-105
Gloucester, 2, 6, 8, 65
Gloucestershire, 3, 5, 9
Golden Valley, 17
Habricia Cottage, 41-2, 109-13, 126
Haunted House, 16
Hillside, 31, 42, 86-8
Jurassic Way, 4
Kenwood Cottage, 42, 114-116
Kimbury Fort, 4
King Charles' Hill/Lane, 1-2, 6, 15, 33, 42-3, 49
King's Place, 100
Knapp House, 35, 37-9
Linden Cottage, 42, 109-13
Lypiatt Park (Over Lypiatt), 12-13, 17-19, 71
Mercia, 8
Nether Lypiatt, 16
Oakridge, 12
Painswick, 3, 10, 19, 32-3
Pitch, The, 41-2, 53, 81, 112, 121
Redding Wood, 98
Rifleman's, The, 35-6, 37
River Severn, 17, 42
Rodborough Fort, 88
Rose Cottage, 18, 32, 37, 42, 55, 57, 60, 61-71, 73-4, 76, 83-5, 99
Scrubs' Cathedral, 29
Severn Bridge, 31

Slad, 5, 15, 17, 20, 23, 27-8, 30, 31, 34-5, 43, 47, 83, 86, 92, 106, 115, 125, 131
Springfield Cottage, 15, 24, 42, 46, 121-2, 126
Stancombe, 41, 71
Star Inn, 26, 31, 47, 115
Steanbridge, 31, 36, 42-3
Stroud Museum, 6
Stroud, 10, 15, 32-4, 42, 92
Swifts Hill, 2, 9, 30, 35-6, 39-41, 46, 123, 127
Througham, 62-3, 71
Timbercombe, 12
Tranters Hill, 36, 50, 70, 109, 115, 123
Tunley, 89, 118
Under Catswood, 17-18, 89-90, 115, 126
Upper Vatch Mill, 37
Vatch, The, 12, 17, 31, 36-7, 47, 92
Vineyard, The, 76
Wessex, 8-9
Westonbirt, 71, 97
Wick Street, 84
Wittentree Clump, 16, 41-2
Woodside Cottage, 50-51, 123-4
Woolpack, The, 33, 105
Worcester, 11
Wygesty, 12
Yew Tree Cottage, 20, 42, 47, 91-8, 117, 120, 126
Zambia, 74-5